The Apocryphal Gospels: A Very Short Introduction

Very Short Introductions available now:

ACCOUNTING Christopher Nobes
ADVERTISING Winston Fletcher
AFRICAN HISTORY
  John Parker and Richard Rathbone
AGNOSTICISM Robin Le Poidevin
ALEXANDER THE GREAT Hugh Bowden
AMERICAN HISTORY Paul S. Boyer
AMERICAN IMMIGRATION David A. Gerber
AMERICAN POLITICAL PARTIES AND
  ELECTIONS L. Sandy Maisel
AMERICAN POLITICS Richard M. Valelly
THE AMERICAN PRESIDENCY Charles O. Jones
ANAESTHESIA Aidan O'Donnell
ANARCHISM Colin Ward
ANCIENT EGYPT Ian Shaw
ANCIENT GREECE Paul Cartledge
THE ANCIENT NEAR EAST Amanda H. Podany
ANCIENT PHILOSOPHY Julia Annas
ANCIENT WARFARE Harry Sidebottom
ANGELS David Albert Jones
ANGLICANISM Mark Chapman
THE ANGLO-SAXON AGE John Blair
THE ANIMAL KINGDOM Peter Holland
ANIMAL RIGHTS David DeGrazia
THE ANTARCTIC Klaus Dodds
ANTISEMITISM Steven Beller
ANXIETY Daniel Freeman and Jason Freeman
THE APOCRYPHAL GOSPELS Paul Foster
ARCHAEOLOGY Paul Bahn
ARCHITECTURE Andrew Ballantyne
ARISTOCRACY William Doyle
ARISTOTLE Jonathan Barnes
ART HISTORY Dana Arnold
ART THEORY Cynthia Freeland
ASTROBIOLOGY David C. Catling
ATHEISM Julian Baggini
AUGUSTINE Henry Chadwick
AUSTRALIA Kenneth Morgan
AUTISM Uta Frith
THE AVANT GARDE David Cottington
THE AZTECS David Carrasco
BACTERIA Sebastian G. B. Amyes
BARTHES Jonathan Culler
THE BEATS David Sterritt
BEAUTY Roger Scruton
BESTSELLERS John Sutherland
THE BIBLE John Riches
BIBLICAL ARCHAEOLOGY Eric H. Cline
BIOGRAPHY Hermione Lee
THE BLUES Elijah Wald
THE BOOK OF MORMON Terryl Givens
BORDERS Alexander C. Diener and Joshua Hagen
THE BRAIN Michael O'Shea
THE BRITISH CONSTITUTION Martin Loughlin
THE BRITISH EMPIRE Ashley Jackson
BRITISH POLITICS Anthony Wright
BUDDHA Michael Carrithers
BUDDHISM Damien Keown
BUDDHIST ETHICS Damien Keown
CANCER Nicholas James
CAPITALISM James Fulcher
CATHOLICISM Gerald O'Collins
CAUSATION Stephen Mumford and Rani Lill Anjum
THE CELL Terence Allen and Graham Cowling
THE CELTS Barry Cunliffe
CHAOS Leonard Smith
CHILDREN'S LITERATURE Kimberley Reynolds

CHINESE LITERATURE Sabina Knight
CHOICE THEORY Michael Allingham
CHRISTIAN ART Beth Williamson
CHRISTIAN ETHICS D. Stephen Long
CHRISTIANITY Linda Woodhead
CITIZENSHIP Richard Bellamy
CIVIL ENGINEERING David Muir Wood
CLASSICAL LITERATURE William Allan
CLASSICAL MYTHOLOGY Helen Morales
CLASSICS Mary Beard and John Henderson
CLAUSEWITZ Michael Howard
CLIMATE Mark Maslin
THE COLD WAR Robert McMahon
COLONIAL AMERICA Alan Taylor
COLONIAL LATIN AMERICAN
  LITERATURE Rolena Adorno
COMEDY Matthew Bevis
COMMUNISM Leslie Holmes
COMPLEXITY John H. Holland
THE COMPUTER Darrel Ince
THE CONQUISTADORS Matthew Restall and
  Felipe Fernández-Armesto
CONSCIENCE Paul Strohm
CONSCIOUSNESS Susan Blackmore
CONTEMPORARY ART Julian Stallabrass
CONTEMPORARY FICTION Robert Eaglestone
CONTINENTAL PHILOSOPHY Simon Critchley
CORAL REEFS Charles Sheppard
COSMOLOGY Peter Coles
CRITICAL THEORY Stephen Eric Bronner
THE CRUSADES Christopher Tyerman
CRYPTOGRAPHY Fred Piper and Sean Murphy
THE CULTURAL REVOLUTION
  Richard Curt Kraus
DADA AND SURREALISM David Hopkins
DARWIN Jonathan Howard
THE DEAD SEA SCROLLS Timothy Lim
DEMOCRACY Bernard Crick
DERRIDA Simon Glendinning
DESCARTES Tom Sorell
DESERTS Nick Middleton
DESIGN John Heskett
DEVELOPMENTAL BIOLOGY Lewis Wolpert
THE DEVIL Darren Oldridge
DIASPORA Kevin Kenny
DICTIONARIES Lynda Mugglestone
DINOSAURS David Norman
DIPLOMACY Joseph M. Siracusa
DOCUMENTARY FILM Patricia Aufderheide
DREAMING J. Allan Hobson
DRUGS Leslie Iversen
DRUIDS Barry Cunliffe
EARLY MUSIC Thomas Forrest Kelly
THE EARTH Martin Redfern
ECONOMICS Partha Dasgupta
EDUCATION Gary Thomas
EGYPTIAN MYTH Geraldine Pinch
EIGHTEENTH-CENTURY BRITAIN Paul Langford
THE ELEMENTS Philip Ball
EMOTION Dylan Evans
EMPIRE Stephen Howe
ENGELS Terrell Carver
ENGINEERING David Blockley
ENGLISH LITERATURE Jonathan Bate
ENVIRONMENTAL ECONOMICS Stephen Smith
EPIDEMIOLOGY Rodolfo Saracci
ETHICS Simon Blackburn

Paul Foster

THE APOCRYPHAL GOSPELS

A Very Short Introduction

OXFORD
UNIVERSITY PRESS

OXFORD
UNIVERSITY PRESS

Great Clarendon Street, Oxford OX2 6DP

Oxford University Press is a department of the University of Oxford.
It furthers the University's objective of excellence in research, scholarship,
and education by publishing worldwide in

Oxford New York

Auckland Cape Town Dar es Salaam Hong Kong Karachi
Kuala Lumpur Madrid Melbourne Mexico City Nairobi
New Delhi Shanghai Taipei Toronto

With offices in

Argentina Austria Brazil Chile Czech Republic France Greece
Guatemala Hungary Italy Japan Poland Portugal Singapore
South Korea Switzerland Thailand Turkey Ukraine Vietnam

Oxford is a registered trade mark of Oxford University Press
in the UK and in certain other countries

Published in the United States
by Oxford University Press Inc., New York

© Paul Foster 2009

The moral rights of the author have been asserted
Database right Oxford University Press (maker)

First published 2009

All rights reserved. No part of this publication may be reproduced,
stored in a retrieval system, or transmitted, in any form or by any means,
without the prior permission in writing of Oxford University Press,
or as expressly permitted by law, or under terms agreed with the appropriate
reprographics rights organization. Enquiries concerning reproduction
outside the scope of the above should be sent to the Rights Department,
Oxford University Press, at the address above

You must not circulate this book in any other binding or cover
and you must impose the same condition on any acquirer

British Library Cataloguing in Publication Data

Data available

Library of Congress Cataloging in Publication Data

Data available

Typeset by SPI Publisher Services, Pondicherry, India
Printed in Great Britain by
Ashford Colour Press Ltd, Gosport, Hampshire

ISBN 978-0-19-923694-7

9 10

Contents

List of Illustrations

Chapter 1

The apocryphal gospels – what's in a name?

> There are also many other things which Jesus did; were every one
> of them to be written, I suppose that the world itself could not
> contain the books that would be written.
>
> (John 21.25)

So ends the Gospel of John, with an acknowledgement that it
contained only a limited number of the traditions about Jesus. But is
this statement mere authorial hyperbole, or does it reflect a reality
that in the gospel writer's day there was a vast number of stories and
sayings attributed to Jesus in circulation? If, even to a limited extent,
the author of the fourth gospel portrays the prevailing circumstances
of his own day, it becomes fascinating to ask what happened to all
these extra traditions concerning Jesus. In all likelihood the vagaries
of ancient history would mean the vast majority were lost in the mists
of time. Romantic notions of such material surviving through long
chains of oral tradition reaching down two millennia are simply
fanciful. For such additional traditions to survive, the only plausible
mechanism would be through the medium of written texts: either
copied and transmitted by scribes down through the centuries, or
through the chance preservation of ancient manuscripts.

Up until about the 1870s, only the first of these two alternatives
was known to have led to the preservation of extra-biblical

traditions concerning Jesus. Manuscripts recounting stories purporting to be events in the life of Jesus before his public ministry, or further post-crucifixion narratives, were generally the types of documents that had survived through scribal copying. Hence the written sources tended to be medieval or early-modern copies, many centuries removed from the date of composition of these extra-biblical stories. In many ways these represented a 'gap-filling' exercise, by providing details of the so-called 'hidden years' of Jesus' life.

However, during the last quarter of the 19th century, as archaeologists commenced large-scale excavations in Egypt and scholars began trawling through dusty library collections, long-buried and long-forgotten manuscripts started to emerge. The first discovery, made in 1885, was a relatively small scrap of six incomplete lines of text found amongst the papyrus collection of Archduke Rainer in Vienna. Whether this text is actually part of a separate, larger, previously unknown gospel, or is simply a variant reading of part of the Gospel of Mark, is contested. Nonetheless, it was the first window on the murky world of the transmission of ancient non-canonical Christian texts. A more substantial discovery was unearthed at an archaeological dig at Akhmîm in Upper Egypt during the winter season of 1886/7 by members of a French team. A small book, or codex, was exhumed from a monk's grave and this contained 4 texts in its 66 pages. The first, ranging over 9 pages, was identified as a fragment of the lost text the *Gospel of Peter*, which had previously been known only by name, having been discussed by various early Christian writers. The rapid stream of discoveries continued through the last decade of the 19th century.

In 1897, two young Oxford scholars, B. P. Grenfell and A. S. Hunt, commenced an archaeological dig at an Egyptian village called el-Behesna, some 100 miles south of Cairo and 10 miles west of the Nile. The village name stems from the Arab period and did in fact represent the renaming of what had been a much larger city known as Oxyrhynchus. As is the case now, when Grenfell and Hunt

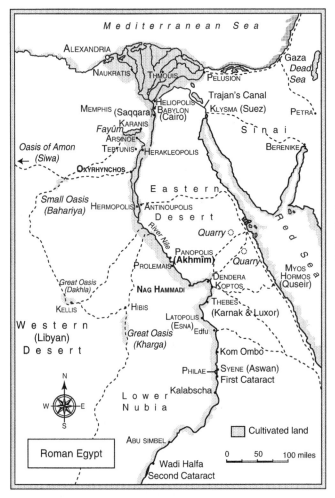

1. This map shows the location of three important manuscript discoveries in Egypt: Akhmîm, Nag Hammadi, and Oxyrhynchus

arrived at Oxyrhynchus little remained of that ancient settlement apart from one stone column – and various rubbish heaps, each about 30 feet deep. The mixed debris of those rubbish heaps contained a vast number of papyrus fragments – basically what turned out to be the waste paper of the day. This contained a fascinating array of documents, including tax receipts, bills of sale, personal letters, and census records. Such finds were the so-called 'documentary papyri' that provide such vivid insights into the everyday lives of people from the various social strata of that ancient society. Combined, however, with such documents were literary texts. Fragments of Homer and schoolboy exercises in copying Euripides were found, along with various Christian texts. Apart from ecclesial texts and fragments of writings contained in the Bible, new texts were discovered that purported to record the actual words of Jesus or those of his followers. In fact, the very first text from the Oxyrhynchus trove to be published was entitled *Sayings of Our Lord* and contained both previously unattested sayings and versions of sayings that varied from the parallels in biblical texts. It would only later transpire that these fragments were part of a larger text known under the title of the *Gospel of Thomas*. However, what this series of early discoveries did was to open up the possibility that an alternative source of traditions about Jesus existed and that this might offer a radically different insight into the teachings and person of Jesus. From these early discoveries, scholars collected together these disparate texts and published collections of 'apocryphal', or 'non-canonical', gospel texts. They shared in common the fact that they were not included among the biblical writings. Thus a new sub-branch of investigation into early Christianity began to emerge – the study of the apocryphal New Testament.

The meaning of the term 'apocryphal gospels'

The very title 'apocryphal gospels' is a highly contested label. Taking the word 'gospel' first, it may be thought that it is self-evident what this term means. Depending on the definition

4

2. Oxyrhynchus – excavation of 'rubbish' mounds at this site led to the discovery of between a quarter to half a million papyrus fragments. Fewer than 6,000 of these have been published at the time of writing

3. An image of the original excavation at Oxyrhynchus. Children were often employed for the delicate work because of their more careful handling of the papyri, and their body-weight made less impact on the mounds

employed, the meaning of the word 'gospel' may appear obvious. A recent writer commenting on the *Gospel of Judas* stated that this work does not deserve the label 'gospel' since, according to the author in question, it says nothing about the 'real' Jesus. From this perspective, the definition of the term 'gospel' appears to become little more than a shorthand way of referring to writings about Jesus that were later deemed to be 'orthodox'. In other words, the term is narrowly and exclusively defined as referring to one of the four gospels contained in the canonical New Testament. Such circular thinking automatically excludes from the discussion those texts which some early Christians may have considered authoritative, even of equal value alongside the 'four Gospels' that are instantly recognizable today. These additional texts need to be taken on their own terms and judged against the historical background in which they were written, rather than being excluded on the basis of anachronistic and theologically motivated criteria.

Returning to the term 'gospel', it is important to understand that this word had a range of meanings even before it came to be used as a term for designating written texts about Jesus. There are basically two sources of evidence which help to clarify the meaning of the Greek word group relating to 'gospel' (the noun, *euangelion* = 'gospel', and the verb *euangelizō* = 'to announce glad tidings/to proclaim good news') prior to its use to designate early Christian texts that employed the term as a title. The first comes from the Greek translation of the Old Testament scriptures known as the Septuagint. In that collection of texts, this word group refers to an oral proclamation or the announcement of some news. Often the news is a positive event (Isa. 52.7; Nah. 2.1). However, this is not uniformly the case. In one Old Testament story, a messenger thinking that he is bringing 'good news' to David of King Saul's death soon learns that David does not consider this as glad tidings. The unfortunate herald pays the ultimate price for being unable to distinguish between good and bad news (2 Sam. 4.10)! The second source of evidence does not emerge from biblical material, but rather from the use of the term in association with the imperial cult. The Jewish historian Josephus, who skilfully advanced his own career by predicting Vespasian's rise to imperial office, wrote of the effect of the proclamation of the new emperor taking office in AD 69 at the culmination of one of the most turbulent years in Roman history: 'Every city kept festival for good news [*euangelia*] and offered sacrifices on his behalf' (*Jewish War* IV.618). In the so-called Priene inscription. The laudatory language that describes Augustus refers to the consequences of his ascension and reign in the following manner; It is 'resulting in signalling to the world through him the good news [*euangelion*] of the birthday of our god' (lines 40–1).

Therefore, it is unsurprising that in the earliest stages of the Jesus movement, the term 'gospel' denoted an oral proclamation of some event of significance, usually with positive ramifications – such as the accession of a new emperor. Christian usage of 'gospel' language may have looked to the antecedents in the Old Testament, but would also have been attuned to the popular contemporary usage as part of the imperial cult, especially in the eastern Mediterranean where emperor veneration appeared to flourish. If this were the case, then Paul's appropriation of 'gospel' language was far from a politically neutral manoeuvre. Rather, in a subversive and controversial manner the one who styled himself as 'apostle to the gentiles' intentionally took hold of the language of the imperial cult in order to claim that Christ, not Caesar, was the source of good news and the manifestation of divinity.

So if the term 'gospel' started its Christian phase as referring to oral announcements, why, how, and when did it come to be associated with written documents? Perhaps the first two aspects of the question are somewhat easier to answer – at least partially. As the numbers of first-generation followers of Jesus diminished, there was presumably a need to enshrine community tradition in order to preserve and communicate the message. It is almost certain that the content of early forms of written tradition was derived from oral proclamations known as 'gospel'. The earliest of the canonical gospels, that written by Mark, opens with the words 'Beginning of the gospel of Jesus Christ...' (Mark 1.1). So it appears that as early believers began to crystallize what had previously existed as an oral proclamation into a written form, the same term 'gospel' was used to describe the content of the written message. However, the title of this literary work, either simply 'according to Mark' or 'the Gospel according to Mark', was almost certainly not part of the text when it first circulated. It was, therefore, a striking change for a term that was used to describe oral proclamations to be applied as a description of a written work, especially given the presumably significant differences in content. So when did this relabelling first occur? Like many innovations, its originator and the specific circumstances that led to this daring use of terminology are unknown, but texts written by Christian figures in the 2nd century use the term 'gospel' to refer to written documents as though this terminology was widely understood and was a common way to refer to the type of documents under discussion.

The 'hard evidence' for the earliest demonstrable use of the term 'gospel' to designate a written form rather than an oral proclamation comes from two sources. First, the earliest manuscripts of the writings with titles using the term 'gospel' date to around the year AD 200 and the decades that follow. An early copy of the papyrus manuscript of the Gospel of John known as P^{66} dated at some point around the end of the 2nd century has the title 'Gospel according to John'; the slightly later manuscript containing both Luke and John (P^{75}) has a title at the end of Luke stating 'Gospel according to Luke' and then at the beginning of John, 'Gospel according to John'. Thus, while there may not have been consensus even in the same manuscript concerning whether such titles belonged at the beginning or the end of the text, these writings were already being labelled as 'gospels'.

The second piece of evidence is even earlier. Writing around AD 180, Irenaeus, the bishop of Lyon, in his work *Adversus Haeresus*

('Against Heresies') refers on multiple occasions to written documents using the term 'gospel'. In book 3 of this work, he refers to the four evangelists issuing 'gospels' in different geographical locations – although the location of Luke's Gospel is not specified (*Ad. Haer.* 3.1.1). Irenaeus uses the term 'gospel' to denote written documents unambiguously on many occasions and without explanation. The very fact that he offers no explanation leads to the supposition that he was not the innovator of this usage, and the natural way in which he uses such terminology suggests that 'gospel' as a designation for a written document had been established for some time. While certain scholars have argued for such usage stemming back to the beginning of the 2nd century, such a claim cannot be established with any certainty. Rather, it appears more accurate to state simply that by the second half of the 2nd century Christian writers could quite naturally speak of certain written documents as 'gospels'.

The designation of those gospels outside the fourfold collection as 'apocryphal' is a description that originated with post-Enlightenment scholars. Although this remains a common way of referring to such texts, the term can carry negative associations. Thus it may be preferable to call such texts 'non-canonical', thereby simply distinguishing them from the four gospels that formed part of the canon of the New Testament at a later stage in history. It must be remembered that the distinction between 'canonical' and 'non-canonical' texts is anachronistic, in that it did not apply at the time when the texts were written. Such a separation was possible only a few centuries later when a fixed list of New Testament texts began to emerge. Although recognizing the limitations of terms such as 'apocryphal' or 'non-canonical', both these labels will be used to refer to the range of gospels under discussion. This approach recognizes the fact that this has become the common designation, but behind such shorthand labels it needs to be seen that these are imposed modern categories that were not used by Christians in the 2nd and 3rd centuries when many of these texts were being produced or circulated.

How many gospels are there?

Irenaeus not only provides the earliest certain usage of the term 'gospel' to refer to written documents, he also gives the first extant reference to the existence of a fourfold gospel collection. While he asserts that there is only one gospel (i.e. the central message of Christianity), he also declares that it is known and received in a fourfold form and he explicitly names Matthew, Mark, Luke, and John as the authors of the four documents (*Ad. Haer.* 3.11.8). This may seem to settle the debate about the number of gospels. However, it is well known that the writing of history is dominated by the perspectives of those who are victorious in battles over territory or ideas. Irenaeus' position anticipates what was to become the received orthodoxy of 4th-century Christianity, yet even his complex arguments against competing views subvert his claim that it is self-evident that there can be no more or no fewer than four gospels.

In the process of refuting the followers of Valentinus, Irenaeus accuses them of 'possessing more gospels than there really are' (*Ad. Haer.* 3.11.9). He goes on to name one such document, the 'Gospel of Truth', but argues that this is so discrepant from the four 'received' gospels that it should not be classed in the same way. Despite his protestations, this argument vividly betrays the fact that for other Christians in the 2nd century there were indeed other gospels than the four sanctioned by Irenaeus. For those who read such 'alternative' writings, these documents were not of a lesser standing, but could be read as authoritative texts disclosing divine revelation. Other early Church figures reveal knowledge of documents bearing the title 'gospel' which do not belong to the corpus of the fourfold gospel. For instance, the 4th-century Church historian Eusebius of Caesarea recounts the story of Serapion, bishop of Antioch, visiting the town of Rhossos in his diocese. While there, he became acquainted with a document known as the *Gospel of Peter*. Initially he stated no objection to this 'gospel' being read alongside the four received gospels. However, on his return to Antioch, advisors instructed him that some form of this text was used by a group known as the Docetics – deemed to be heretics. Consequently, Serapion wrote to the church in Rhossos rescinding his earlier permission to use this text (Eusebius, *H.E.* 6.12.1–6). In addition to numerous examples of early Christian writers mentioning the names of texts containing the word 'gospel' in the title, there are also manuscripts of non-canonical gospels that occur with titles bearing the term 'gospel'. It is difficult to enumerate how many texts, disputed or otherwise, might be described as gospels since some are categorized because of their form rather than an explicit title, but recent attempts would perhaps list around 40 distinct ancient texts in this category.

Unless a restrictive canonical approach is adopted that allows only the fourfold collection to be labelled as 'gospels', there is obviously a greater number of texts that potentially could be included in this category. The problem arises in deciding what to include or exclude. Upon reading the text, it is perhaps possible to sympathize with Irenaeus' refutation of the 'Gospel of Truth' as being a gospel. On the likely assumption that the text of the same title discovered at Nag Hammadi is the document to which Irenaeus refers, then it must be admitted that it does not read like one of the familiar four canonical texts. However, this text, like the Gospel of Mark, uses the term 'gospel' in its opening phrase, and this is no doubt intended as an important clue as to how its contents are to be understood. Presumably such a designation was not problematic for those early Christians who read it.

On the other hand, there are texts that, in the form in which they survive, do not bear the word 'gospel' in their title, such as the infancy account attributed to Thomas or the *Gospel of Peter* (although Christian writers refer to texts known by these titles), but nonetheless they do convey traditions and teachings of Jesus. Perhaps the best strategy is to investigate various texts as 'gospel-type' writings. These writings would include texts that designate themselves as 'gospels' either through a title or description of contents. The selection also includes untitled writings that may be identified with titles of 'gospel writings' known by early Christian writers (an example would be the *Gospel of Peter*). Furthermore, it is helpful to consider those writings such as the *Protevangelium of James*, which has been labelled as a 'gospel' by scholarly convention rather than ancient attribution. Admittedly, this may cast a very wide net, and the grouping is functional rather than strictly defined, but the benefit in at least considering such a wide range of potential gospel texts is that it enriches the understanding of the diversity of this category in early Christianity and beyond, and seeks to ensure that texts are not excluded on the basis of preconceived theological boundaries.

It is therefore necessary to be aware of different types of gospel texts that circulated in the ancient world. As different texts are discussed here, some of these gospels will be seen to be narrative accounts, others will catalogue sayings of Jesus, while still other texts concern not the adult ministry of Jesus but his childhood or even his mother's birth. At the other end of the chronological spectrum, a number of gospel texts purportedly record discourses that occurred after the resurrection with figures privileged to receive such revelatory instruction.

Gnosticism: misnomer or helpful category?

Many of the alternative gospels that have come to light in recent manuscript finds, or those documents named as gospels by early Christian writers, were labelled either descriptively or pejoratively as 'Gnostic'. One trend in recent scholarship has been to question the utility of this term, arguing that it is both too broad and also repeatedly misused. It has been suggested that such labelling is not only unhelpful, but actually misleading. Consequently, the total abandonment of the term has been advocated. While some of the criticisms levelled against the use of this term are warranted, especially the labelling of any text with a mystic or cosmological interest as being 'pre-' or 'proto-Gnostic', to abandon the term altogether seems akin to throwing out the proverbial baby with the bathwater and in the process losing a helpful heuristic tool that is of value if correctly understood.

Part of the critique against using the term 'Gnosticism' is that it does not create a useful taxonomy for categorizing the variety of religious movements of the 2nd century that are often grouped under this umbrella. Furthermore, it has been stated that the label 'Gnosticism' is a modern construct, unknown to the ancients, and that there was no such thing as a coherent Gnostic religion in the 2nd century. It is indeed true that there was no unified Gnostic religion in this period. Then again, neither was there any monolithic or clearly defined and governed Christianity – especially in the first half of the 2nd century. Despite what later succession lists suggest, there was no papal figure occupying episcopal office in Rome. Instead, Christianity, even in the imperial capital, was at best a loose confederacy of house churches for much of the 2nd century, and at worst it was a collection of competing groups disputing the way to express their devotion to the Christ figure. In response to such observations, those who reject the category of Gnosticism would tend to argue that by contrast Christianity was not only a self-designation in the contemporary Greek vocabulary of the early centuries of the movement, but that it represents a phenomenon that has had a continuous existence since then, whereas Gnosticism seems to have disappeared by the end of the 5th century and is not spoken of again until the post-Enlightenment period. In this regard, it may be comparable to the use of the term 'Charismatic' to describe the 'religion' of various groups that have widely divergent practices but nonetheless share a belief that ecstatic Spirit-led experiences distinguish them from the wider category of Christians.

Similarly, 'Gnosticism' as used here does not refer to a fully thought-out belief system, or to a coherent and well-developed 'religion'. Rather, it is intended as a useful shorthand way of denoting a collection of groups with some highly significant differences, but unified by some strikingly similar features. Although there is debate as to whether Gnostic thought pre-dates Christianity, without offering any judgement on that issue here the term will be used to refer only to those texts that attempt a synthesis of developed cosmology with some form of the Jesus tradition. First, these groups understand the created realm to have been brought into existence by a 'demiurge' – a mediator figure who is below the all-high and fully spiritual God. This device preserves the taint of the material realm from contaminating the spiritual sphere. Consequently, the demiurge is an intermediary to whom responsibility for the creation of the earth can be ascribed, and this in turn protects the supreme divinity of the spiritual realm from contact with what is conceived as being the defiling physical sphere. Second, there is a sustained interest in rites of ascent that allowed initiates to return to the higher spiritual realm. Third, those who adhered to such ideas should not be seen as a well-formed and hermetically discrete entity removed from wider Christianity. Instead, the devotees of Gnosticism are probably best thought of as being elitist early Christians who co-existed alongside proto-orthodox Christians but claimed superior insight into the mythological and deeper spiritual reality of the Christ-redeemer figure.

There is also diversity within the wider category of Gnosticism, which can be clarified by a range of subcategories. Taking its name from its supposed foundational figure Valentinus, Valentinian Gnosticism had perhaps the least developed cosmology and deviated least from emergent orthodoxy. Nonetheless its divergences are striking. It advocated a belief in various aeons, or emanations from God. The first series consisted of 30 aeons, or 15 complementary male and female pairs. People were seen as being comprised of both a spiritual female angelic part and a material male human part. The reunion of the fractured being could only be achieved through participation in Valentinian rituals, and ascent through the realms of the various aeons. A key text for understanding the wider theological perspective of Valentinianism is the *Gospel of Truth*, to be discussed in the next chapter.

Valentinus, the person with whom the origin of the Valentinian thought system is linked, remains a shadowy and allusive figure to modern enquirers. The little that can be patched together of his life suggests that Valentinus was an influential and respected intellectual teacher in Rome who received his own training in the academic hothouse of Alexandria. He appears to have arrived in Rome around AD 140 where he was a prominent teacher for approximately 15 years. After this he most likely moved to Cyprus, where he continued his teaching activity. During the period of Valentinus' sojourn in Rome, two other leading Christian intellectuals were operating in the imperial capital: Marcion, with his radical revisionist approach to the Jewish origins of Christianity which sought to jettison any links the new movement had with the God of the Old Testament; and Justin Martyr, an intellectual apologist for Christianity who presented the outlook of the new religion in philosophical terms in order to defend it from the charge of being a flimsy and folkloric movement. Although judged by the perspective of history in markedly different ways, these three figures shared much in common as they attempted to offer robust presentations of Christianity.

It is perhaps noteworthy that around this time, the middle of the 2nd century, in Rome, much of the impetus and leadership came from independent teachers who attracted groups of students. There does not appear to have been any centralized authority figure, rather as in the mid-1st century the system of loosely connected house churches seems to have prevailed. Therefore the notion of a succession of bishops of Rome, tracing their lineage back to Peter, appears to be a construct of later Church history and is not representative of the first 100 years or so of Christianity in Rome.

It was amid this charged and rarified atmosphere that intellectuals such as Valentinus, who had been attracted by the person and teachings of Jesus, tried to offer an articulate and rigorous exposition of the Christian faith. It is unfortunate that only a few fragments of his own works survive, and then usually embedded in the writings of his opponents. Yet even those who disagree with his theology acknowledge his 'brilliant mind' (Jerome, *In Hos.* 2.10) or the beauty of his poetic language (Tertullian, *De Carne* 17). The influence of Platonic thinking on Valentinus is obvious both in the preserved fragments and the comments made by those writing against him. This is also to be understood against the wider backdrop of a renaissance of philosophical thinking in the 2nd century usually known as the Second Sophistic. Such a revival and return to the great philosophical writers of 4th-century BC Athens also explains why one finds a fragment of Plato's *Republic* as one of the texts in the sixth Nag Hammadi codex. Concepts and ideas borrowed from Plato shaped the thinking of Valentinus, and a cosmology was developed that longed for the soul's deliverance from the constraints of the material realm. While certain texts at Nag Hammadi have been identified as Valentinian, it is uncertain how many of these were written by Valentinus. Instead, the majority appear to have been penned by his followers. Those who adhered to this form of Christianity were perhaps part of an emerging leisured and socially privileged wing of the Church in Rome which, while not representing the majority of Christians, perhaps because of their affluence and status had a disproportional influence on their own local gatherings. While the *Gospel of Philip* is but one text to emerge from this Valentinian environment, its compendious nature means that it gives various snapshots of key theological ideas and liturgical rites that were practised by Valentinian adherents.

Sethian Gnosticism takes its name not from the movement's intellectual founder, but from Seth, the third son of Adam and Eve, who plays an important role in the theology of the Sethians. This form of Gnosticism, with its strong Jewish elements, is often seen as having intellectual origins prior to Christianity. Hence it is suggested that it was formed from an intermingling of Jewish and

Platonic ideas. While this is debatable, the key texts that are usually seen as reflecting Sethianism, such as the *Apocryphon of John*, the *Coptic Gospel of the Egyptians*, and the *Gospel of Judas*, are, as they stand, Christian writings which depict their similar cosmogonies through the eyes of figures known from the New Testament. The origin of Seth is seen as being the result of a divine incarnation. In this sense, Seth is more closely tied to the spiritual realm than are the descendants of Cain. Consequently the strand of humanity which is derived from Seth is superior spiritual stock, and the spiritual seed within such individuals leads them to participate in the veneration of Seth and to strive for the upward journey of the soul so that it may return to the realm from where Seth descended. The theological system adopts a *via negative* in describing the ultimate divine being as invisible, intangible, and ineffable. Thus the transcendence of God who defies human categorization is a significant, although not unique, feature of Sethian thought.

Ophite Gnosticism is best known through the writings of early Christian figures who opposed the outlook of the group. Akin to other forms of Gnosticism, its belief system also looked for the upward ascent of the soul through the various spheres of the archons. Such a journey was possible only for the enlightened soul who had become the possessor of certain mantras of magical words that allowed progress to the next higher level. Origen, the learned 3rd-century writer, states that their system of thought had been diagrammatically represented and that he himself had obtained a copy of this diagram, with great difficulty. Various attempts have been made to understand this pictogram from Origen's written description, and while there is consensus surrounding many features, the finer details are disputed. What the diagram depicts, as it is described, is a series of linked and concentric circles representing the multiple spheres that might be encountered in the soul's journey. Again a fundamental feature is the ascent of the soul as it escapes the material world and returns to its pristine spiritual state.

Although it is necessary to be aware of many of the partially valid criticisms that have been levelled against using the term 'Gnosticism', nonetheless it remains the most convenient and helpful umbrella term for categorizing a range of diverse religious expressions of Christianity that taught complex mythologies and cosmologies. Within this wider category a number of branches can be identified, as we have described. These share many ideas and are not totally separate systems of thought. Thus a text may have multiple features, and these may not uniformly represent just one sub-branch of Gnosticism. As mentioned, there is an ongoing debate concerning the existence of a pre-Christian form of 'Gnosticism'. In part, this is due to the identification of significant Jewish elements in a number of texts. Since some of the motifs appear closer to internal Jewish exegetical questions, and are not discussed in Christian contexts apart from Gnostic texts, it has been suggested that there was an original Gnostic religion which pre-dated Christianity, but was at a later point subsumed by that new religious movement. However, despite trawling evidence from various potentially related traditions, such as Mandaic and Manichaean texts, there has been no compelling evidence of a developed form of 'Gnosticism' prior to Christianity. Consequently, despite the discovery of new texts many scholars 'have remained unconvinced that they demonstrate the existence of a fully-fledged Gnosticism with a redeemer myth prior to Christianity'. For this reason, here the label 'Gnostic' will be used to denote Christian Gnostic texts that begin to surface from the 2nd century onwards.

The rediscovery of the non-canonical gospels

Most of the non-canonical gospels, if they were known at all throughout the Middle Ages and early-modern period, were known only by name. As has been mentioned, this changed dramatically from the late 19th century onwards. The dry and desiccating conditions of Upper Egypt had provided the ideal climate for the preservation of papyrus documents. The Oxyrhynchus find was perhaps the most spectacular discovery of ancient texts. Grenfell and Hunt found mounds 30 feet deep containing a mixture of rubbish, earth, and precious papyrus texts. These were excavated by Egyptian labourers, piled in baskets, and then boxed and sent back to Oxford. One papyrus roll was protected in a Huntley and Palmer's biscuit tin, others were shipped in tea chests. The volume of this find is hard to quantify, but around a quarter to half a million papyrus fragments were discovered. Texts unearthed over a 100 years ago are still being sorted, edited, and published. A count shows that at the time of writing, 73 volumes of published texts have appeared, containing transcriptions and analyses of nearly 5,000 documents – somewhere between 2% and 4% of the texts.

Just over half a century was to pass before the next large cache of writings was discovered. However, during the intervening period some discoveries of individual texts came to light. During the first half of the 1930s, the so-called 'Unknown Gospel' – Papyrus Egerton 2 – was purchased from an antiquities dealer by the British Museum. At the time, the text caused quite a stir since its dating to the middle of the 2nd century meant that it was then viewed as the oldest surviving Christian manuscript. It was considered startling that such a divergent text should go back to the earliest generations of the Christian movement and, at the time of its discovery, should pre-date all surviving manuscripts of any text in the New Testament. Although not quite as ancient, the next huge find occurred again in Egypt, where the climatic conditions had proved so favourable to manuscript preservation, shortly after the end of the Second World War. Located in Middle Egypt, Nag Hammadi (the anglicized form of its Arabic name) is a small town of some 30,000 inhabitants located 80 kilometres northwest of Luxor, known as Chenoboskian in classical antiquity. Unearthed at the foot of a cliff, a local farm hand made one of the most interesting manuscript discoveries for casting light on a distinctive branch of early Christianity. More of the details of this spectacular and dangerous discovery will be outlined in the next chapter. Suffice to mention that the find comprised of 12 leather-bound

4. Bernard P. Grenfell (right) and Arthur S. Hunt (left), the two young scholars from Queen's College, Oxford, led the excavation of the Oxyrhynchus site. They were entrusted with this task, which was funded by the Egypt Exploration Society, in all likelihood because more senior scholars were either more interested in pharoanic Egypt or considered the task unlikely to yield substantial results

papyrus codices, along with pages torn from a 13th book, buried in a sealed jar. The texts in these books contain, among other things, a mixture of esoteric and mystical Christian thinking, apocalyptic visions, a fragment of Plato's *Republic*, and a similarly broken and truncated version of the *Sentences of Sextus* – a widely circulating text in the late antique and medieval periods providing moral instruction. Such diversity reflects the eclectic reading tastes of those who were probably elite early Christians, perhaps continuing to exist within mainstream Christianity.

Manuscripts have continued to come to light in the 21st century. Although acquired in 1961 by the Egyptian Museum of Berlin, and accessioned as Papyrus Berolinensis 22220, the nature of this text did not become known until 1991, when the sheets of manuscript were first worked on for conservation purposes. The text was first published in 1999 and given the title *Gospel of the Savior* by its editors. The text known as the *Gospel of Judas* first became widely known only in 2006, although the codex of which it was a part appears to have first been discovered in a tomb in Middle Egypt as early as 1978. From here it passed through the murky and illicit world of antiquities dealers, finally being purchased by the Maecenas Foundation in Switzerland in 2001, when scholarly work began on the restoration of the codex, which had been badly mishandled since its discovery. At one point it appears to have been frozen, in the mistaken belief that this would assist preservation. Quite the opposite was the case – and the structure of this codex and its brittle pages were severely damaged. Thanks to the skilled work of a team of manuscript restorers, much of its contents were expertly pieced together, but even so large parts of what was apparently a near complete codex when discovered have been irrevocably lost.

The significance of the apocryphal gospels

Exaggerated claims are often made concerning the non-canonical gospels that often leave scholars shaking their collective heads. Reports are not infrequent that suggest that a new discovery is sensational, earth-shattering, or heralds the end of Christianity. The basic problem with such claims is that they try to make a textual discovery say something about a period well before the text was written. In particular, there is a failure to see the majority of these texts as products of the 2nd and 3rd centuries, with little historical relevance for answering questions about the historical Jesus of 1st-century Judaea. Instead, since they often react against ecclesial hierarchies and institutional religion, these recently recovered texts can be seen as a vehicle for repristinating the image of Jesus in a way that not only makes him a radical figure, but also a highly mystical one who resonates with modern spiritual tastes. The problems that beset the project of recovering an accurate portrait of the historical Jesus from the canonical gospels are well known. These difficulties become no less acute in relation to non-canonical texts. In fact, in many ways they are exacerbated by greater historical distance, a worldview that refracts the teaching of Jesus through the lens of a multilayered understanding of the heavens through which the soul must ascend to recapture its true divine nature, and through allowing ecstatic visionary experience to predominate over the maintenance of tradition. The New Testament itself is not free from such problems, although perhaps some of its texts are not affected to the same degree as some of the apocryphal writings, which are even more heavily overlaid with developing theological concerns. Having said this, what then is the value of the non-canonical gospels, and why bother reading such texts?

Primarily these texts say much concerning the diversity and vibrancy of those groups in the 2nd and 3rd centuries which claimed to stand in continuity with the Jesus movement of the 1st century. Given the radically divergent ways in which the core allegiance to Jesus could be expressed, such fluidity at the earliest stages of development should prompt extreme caution about interpreting Christianity as a monolithic and doctrinally unified form from which Gnostics, Docetics, and a host of other 'heretics' diverged. It appears far more accurate to speak of divergent and at times competing strands which sought to promote their own perspectives in relation to the significance of Jesus. While it is perhaps tempting to project contemporary concerns and theological questions back onto ancient contexts, such ancient documents may offer some significant resources for discussing current issues as long as it is recognized that they come from a culturally distant society, their perspectives are shaped by pre-scientific understandings, and that the worldviews they encapsulate originate from a pre-Enlightenment mode of thought.

While the texts as 'whole documents' may reflect a period later than the 1st century and thus enshrine the concerns of various Christian groups living in the 2nd and 3rd centuries, nonetheless there remains the possibility that individual sayings or certain accounts may occasionally go back to the life of Jesus. This situation is much the same for the canonical gospels. Perhaps the major significant difference is that the majority of scholars would date the composition of the canonical gospels to the 1st century, whereas the majority of scholars (although with some notable dissenting voices) would date the non-canonical texts in their completed forms to later centuries. While this certainly does not mean the canonical gospels are pristine historical accounts, it does mean that the greater 'historical gap' between the events they purport to report and the time of the writing of the non-canonical gospels should give pause for thought before building too much on their alternative portrayals of Jesus as being of greater historical worth than their canonical counterparts. The process of recovering authentic sayings or deeds of Jesus from the four canonical accounts is a highly contested endeavour. To believe that this is an easier task for the non-canonical reports is frankly naïve. Notwithstanding this important caveat, a number of scholars have felt that it may be possible to recover authentic Jesus sayings from non-canonical sources – in particular from the *Gospel of Thomas*. It is perhaps instructive to consider the findings of one highly controversial attempt to do just this.

The Jesus Seminar was founded by Robert Funk in 1985. Its primary aim was to determine the authentic words of Jesus. Although there have been many other attempts to do this, there had not previously been such a large-scale collaborative enterprise; the Jesus Seminar at its greatest extent grew to a body of more than 200 scholars. By 1993, after bi-annual meetings, the deliberations were completed. Using coloured beads, each scholar cast a vote relating to every saying of Jesus contained in the four canonical gospels and in *Thomas* to indicate their own critical sense of whether the individual saying originated with Jesus. The colours and their designations were as follows: red, Jesus almost certainly said this (or something very similar); pink, Jesus probably said something like this; grey, Jesus did not say this but it reflects his ideas; black, Jesus did not say this and it represents later perspectives or different traditions. Interestingly, of the hundreds of Jesus sayings, the votes of this body of scholars reached the required level for a 'red' saying (0.75 on a scale of 0 to 1.0) in relation to only 15 sayings of Jesus. Admittedly, some of these sayings occurred in more than one gospel so they had multiple attestation, but even counting repeated sayings separately gives only 25 instances of sayings deemed to be unquestionably authentic. Of these 25, 12 occur in Luke, 9 occur in Matthew, 3 in *Thomas*, 1 in Mark, and none in John. Many of the authentic sayings in Matthew and Luke are part of what scholars believe was an early source called Q, which these two gospels are believed to have shared as a written strand of Jesus' sayings. While such statistics may appear shocking to some people, it illustrates the difficulty scholars have in definitively linking any saying contained in either the canonical or non-canonical gospels back to Jesus. Although many would dispute the meagre findings of the Jesus Seminar, and the approach has been widely criticized, often for downplaying the apocalyptic and end-time aspects of Jesus' teaching, the success in bringing together so many scholars to discuss the issue was a major achievement, and very few scholars would claim that it was an easy task to determine authentic Jesus sayings in any strand of the traditions preserved about him in the early Church.

It is for this reason that claims that the non-canonical gospels as a whole reveal an alternative portrait of Jesus free from the theological overlays of a developing 'orthodoxy' must be seen as being false. Admittedly, the early Church developed hierarchical structures and male-dominated forms of leadership, and a number of the non-canonical gospels critique such developments. However, these texts defend the perspectives of their authors and of the communities that read them, but not by presenting a more historically reliable version of the life and teachings of Jesus. Instead, for ideological purposes they create a new way of thinking about salvation, the universe, and the individual's personal search for completeness. In order to critique apostolic Christianity, many of these texts re-invent the story of Jesus, rather than taking readers back to authentic historical bedrock. Thus, the value of these texts must be understood for what it is – a glimpse into the battles fought during the 2nd and 3rd centuries between Christians with radically different understandings of salvation, church order, and the significance of Jesus.

Chapter 2
The 'gospels' from Nag Hammadi

Discovery and publication

The story of the discovery of the 12 bound codices and the remains of a 13th volume at Nag Hammadi is shrouded in intrigue, murder, and revenge. The manuscript collection was unearthed by a fieldworker by the name of Muhammad Ali al-Samman who lived across the Nile from Nag Hammadi in a small hamlet called Qasr. After the sugarcane harvest he was out digging for fertilizer at the base of a nearby cliff. This incident occurred about half a year after the murder of his father in a blood feud. The date of the father's death is recorded in the Nag Hammadi register of deaths as 7 May 1945. Muhammad Ali, although unable to date events by the calendar, was able to remember that the discovery was a few weeks before Coptic Christmas (7 January 1946) and about half a year after his father's death. This makes the likely date of discovery early December 1945.

What Muhammad Ali actually unearthed was a large jar sealed with a bowl that had been attached by bitumen at its opening. In the hope of treasure, he broke the jar open, but he was disappointed to discover only a collection of old books. Apparently he tore some codices up to share among the camel drivers who were present with him. However, the majority declined his offer, so he bundled

5. The site of the discovery of the Nag Hammadi codices, which were unearthed when Muhammad Ali al-Samman was digging for soft soil to use as fertilizer. The books were discovered near Nag Hammadi, between Denderah and Panopolis. The collection of codices had been carefully placed in a tomb in the Pacomian cemetery at the foot of the Djebel el Tarif cliff

them up together again and took them home. These were left in the enclosed courtyard of his house, and it has been reported that his mother burned some of the pages as kindling for the outdoor clay oven. After having attempted to sell the books for about an Egyptian pound or to barter them for some cigarettes, Muhammad Ali was informed by somebody who saw the codices that they were written in Coptic not Arabic. After having deposited Codex III with a Coptic priest, this volume eventually came into the possession of the Coptic Museum in Cairo. Codex I, which turned up in an antique shop and then was smuggled out of Egypt, was finally purchased by the Jung Institute in Zurich and hence became known as the Jung codex. Most of the remaining codices were acquired by a Cypriot antiquities dealer in Cairo, Phocion J. Tano(s).

6. The Nag Hammadi codices. The papyrus sheets were carefully housed in robust leather bindings tied with leather straps

After the application of some pressure, he was persuaded to 'entrust' them to the government. The Egyptian government then nationalized the codices and housed them in the Coptic Museum in Cairo.

During the time immediately after the discovery of the codices, other events took place in Muhammad Ali's life which were personally of greater significance. After the murder of his father in the blood feud, Muhammad Ali's mother had charged her seven sons to keep their mattocks sharpened. The opportunity for revenge came unexpectedly but action was taken swiftly. James Robinson, a leading Nag Hammadi specialist who had direct contact with Muhammad Ali, recorded the recollection of the bloodthirsty attack in the following manner:

> Muhammad Ali's memory of revenge: Someone ran to his house to tell the family that the murderer Aḥmad Īsma*īl was asleep in the heat of the day on a dirty road nearby, with a jug of sugarcane

molasses, the local product, by his side. The sons grabbed their mattocks, fell on the hapless person before he could flee, hacked him up, cut open his heart, and, dividing it up among them, ate it raw, the ultimate act of blood vengeance.

Understandably Muhammad Ali was reluctant to lead Robinson to the site of the discovery after this, since it would take him close to the territory of the family of Aḥmad Īsma*īl and he feared that a further act of blood vengeance would be exacted against him. Robinson sought out the family of Aḥmad Īsma*īl who said they felt that they had exacted revenge when, at a later date, they had opened fire on a funeral cortège involving the family of Muhammad Ali. At this, Muhammad Ali was persuaded to take Robinson to the site where the jar containing the codex had been found.

The story of the discovery took some time to come to light, and the publication of the texts was an equally slow and delayed task. The 1950s was a period of virtual inaction due to political turmoil in Egypt and a lack of impetus from certain academic quarters. It is not fruitful to lay blame or to name individuals involved in this tardy translation and publication process. What should not be entertained is the notion of any conspiracy theory involving the suppression of these texts. Like the Dead Sea Scrolls, there was no Vatican cover-up, simply individual scholars wished to have the glory of publishing as many of the hitherto unknown texts as possible. The surprising thing is that those who had this opportunity in the first decade or two after the discovery did not capitalize on it. Not until the late 1960s did the photographs of the codices begin to filter into the public domain, thanks largely to the semi-clandestine work of James Robinson in reproducing the UNESCO copies of the images at a Paris photographic shop over a single weekend when he had been given access to the files. Facsimile editions were then published at a relatively brisk pace between 1972 and 1977, at which stage the whole corpus was made available in the public domain. Also during 1977, the one-volume edition entitled *The Nag Hammadi Library in English* was published. This brought together the English translations that had appeared in the facsimile volumes. At last scholars could readily consult the entire corpus of texts that had been unearthed some 33 years earlier.

The 'gospel' texts from Nag Hammadi

The question concerning the number of 'gospel' texts discovered among the Nag Hammadi writings is not easily answered. This is not due to fragmentary manuscripts, for on the whole the texts are well preserved, but stems from the difficulty that has been discussed in Chapter 1 of defining what actually is a gospel, and what is not. One helpful clue, at least to the ancient attitude to these texts, is self-reference. Yet as has been mentioned, this can result in too narrow a definition. A number of the documents discovered at Nag Hammadi include the word 'gospel' in self-referential description. Four texts explicitly contain the term 'gospel', either in titles at the beginning or end of the documents, or in the opening sentences – not so much as a title, but as a description of contents.

For pragmatic reasons, in this chapter four Nag Hammadi texts will be discussed: *The Gospel of Thomas*, *The Gospel of Philip*, *The Gospel of Truth*, and *The Gospel of the Egyptians*. Although these have either had the term 'gospel' applied to them, or use the word as a description of their contents, they represent a disparate collection of writings. There are other texts in the Nag Hammadi collection which could also be thought of as gospel-type texts. These include 'revelation dialogues' such as the *Apocryphon of John* or the *Sophia of Jesus Christ*. Although those two texts are not discussed at length in this book, in some ways they share greater similarities in genre with dialogue gospel texts discussed in Chapter 5.

The *Gospel of Thomas*

Amongst the non-canonical gospels, *Thomas* has generated the most interest and offered the greatest prospect of recovering independent early Jesus material outside of the corpus of the four canonical gospels. Although various Greek fragments of *Thomas* were excavated at Oxyrhynchus in 1897 and 1903, it was not until the discovery of the Nag Hammadi codices in 1945 that these fragments could be conclusively identified as part of the *Gospel of Thomas*, and that a thoroughgoing analysis of its theological ideas could be undertaken due to the possession of a fairly complete text. The Nag Hammadi text was written in Coptic (the indigenous language of Egypt which began to be widely used from the 1st century AD and continued until the language was finally replaced by Arabic in the 17th century), and that Coptic version of *Thomas* dates to around the 4th century.

The Coptic text comprises a series of a brief prologue and 114 sayings attributed to the 'living Jesus'. The text opens in the following manner: 'These are the secret words which the living Jesus spoke, and which Didymus Judas Thomas wrote down.' The designation of Jesus as 'living' has occasioned discussion. Various suggestions have been offered. It is possible that the word 'living' is used to denote Jesus in his post-resurrection state – such resurrection dialogues are well known in the corpus of apocryphal writings. Alternatively, it has been noted that the epithet 'living' could be used to indicate that Jesus possesses eternal life and provides such life to others. A more literary variation is to point out that this description represents Jesus as living through his sayings.

Furthermore, the names attributed to the one who wrote down the sayings, 'Didymus Judas Thomas', also require some explanation. Taking these three names in reverse order, first, Thomas is the name used in the canonical gospels for one of Jesus' twelve disciples. While this name occurs only once in the disciple lists of Matthew, Mark, and Luke, it is in the Gospel of John that Thomas gains most prominence, being mentioned on seven occasions. Interestingly, the word 'Thomas' may be related to the Syriac term *t'oma*, meaning 'twin'. Second, the name 'Judas' became stigmatized in early Christianity because of the infamous Judas Iscariot. This meant that those who also possessed this name, especially among the circle of disciples, were distinguished from the betrayer of Jesus either by name changes or the addition of further names. In the Old Syriac version of John's Gospel, in one place where the Greek text refers simply to 'Thomas' the Syriac text describes him as 'Judas Thomas' (John 14.5). Third, the term 'Didymus' is used in John's Gospel to describe Thomas both in John 11.16 and 20.24, as well as in a variant reading at John 14.5. *Didymus* is the Greek word for 'twin'. This means that the notion of Thomas' 'twinship' is heavily and intentionally emphasized by calling him 'Didymus Judas Thomas'. In another non-canonical text, *The Acts of Thomas*, the apostle known as Judas Thomas is identified by a talking colt as 'twin of the Messiah and Apostle of the Most High' (*Acts Thom.* 39). So in one branch of early Christianity, which appears to be centred in Syria, this Thomas who is a twin is in fact the twin (in some way) of Jesus. Such proximity to the foundational figure of Christianity instils the words of Thomas with great authority. This privileged wisdom allows the readers (or probably originally hearers) to enter into a narrative world and access a set of different Jesus traditions, which are not totally unrelated to the four Gospels of the Bible.

Nearly all of the sayings open with the standard phrase 'Jesus said', but Saying 1 is different. It states, 'And he said, "Whoever finds the interpretation of these words will not taste death" ' (*Gos. Thom.* 1). The very fact that this opening saying does not explicitly identify the subject as Jesus lends weight to the suggestion that this is an editorial comment addressed to the readers, instructing them what they must do. However, the

The 'gospels' from Nag Hammadi

7. The end of the text of the *Gospel of Thomas*. As is common
with ancient documents, the title is written at the end of the text. The
Coptic script reads 'The Gospel of Thomas'

means of finding the interpretation of the 'words' that follow is not stated. Presumably for the original readers of this text, authorized meanings would have been discussed within the community that preserved it. It is not until Saying 2 that the actual words of Jesus are unambiguously presented. The second saying states: 'Jesus said, "Whoever seeks, let him not cease seeking until he finds; and when he finds he will be troubled, and when he is troubled he will be amazed, and he will reign over the All." ' Again the emphasis is on the pathway of discovering hidden understanding. Such a saying may align with later Gnostic ideas about privileged knowledge and elitist forms of Christianity. However, since *Thomas* lacks an overarching description of a cosmological system consisting of multilayered heavens, this may well mean that *Thomas* itself did not originate in the context of a well-formed Gnostic belief system, but was attractive to later readers who adhered to those more fully developed cosmologies. The progression that saying outlines, through the stages of being troubled, then amazed, then reigning, suggests that perplexity and confusion are prior stages on a journey of spiritual discovery. There is an important difference between the form of the final clause in the Coptic and Greek versions of this saying. The later Coptic version promises that the 'seeker' addressed in this saying will eventual 'reign over the all'. By contrast, in the Greek version, which although lacunous (i.e. there are some holes in the manuscript) can be reconstructed with a fair degree of certainty, the final clause states 'he will reign, and reigning he will have rest'.

What can be made of these discrepant versions? It appears that the Greek version is original, both on internal grounds and also because Clement of Alexandria (writing around the year AD 200) knows a version of this saying that contains a reference to 'rest'. One option would be to explain the variation as arising from a copyist's or translator's error. The Greek word for 'rest' (ἀναπαήσεται) may perhaps have been misread as 'all' (ἀπάντα), especially if the first word had been split over two lines as it is in the surviving Greek manuscript, with the letters άναπα- written at the end of a line. Such mistakes are not uncommon among scribes working in poor conditions and copying poorly written exemplar texts. However, it may be the case that this change was due to design more than accident. The notion of 'the all' may be related to the concept of the *pleroma*, or the fullness, which becomes important both in certain New Testament Christological formulations (see in particular Col. 1.19; 2.9) as well as in a number of other texts discovered at Nag Hammadi (the *Gospel of Philip* is a noteworthy example). In this case, it is possible that the original text-form has been freely adapted by later users for theological and ideological reasons. The sense of dislocation that may have been experienced by the adherents to exclusivist and marginal communities may have led to a celebration of such an aspirant existence, and this may have been combined with the belief that pursuit of the ascetic life would lead ultimately to reigning over the true cosmic order. In this sense, the potentially alienated audience who read this text may have coped with their sense of dislocation by clinging to the belief that the disturbing ascetic lifestyle they adopted would lead to a higher form of knowledge which would be linked with elevated status in a cosmic reality that they themselves could perceive.

The *Gospel of Thomas* is correctly categorized as a sapiential text, which transmits wise sayings. However, the type of wisdom it contains is not the public or received wisdom that emanates from mainstream sources, such as one finds in the Book of Proverbs. Rather, it comprises veiled and counterintuitive insights that are in essence world-inverting. Jesus can assert that a lion consumed by humans is blessed because it is transformed into humanity (Saying 7), or that the one who understands the world has been transformed into a corpse (Saying 56), or again that money should not be lent for interest but given to those who cannot repay (Saying 99). While it would perhaps be wrong to characterize this text as a 'monastic rule', it does promote a solitary and self-contained existence. Thus in Saying 49, Jesus says: 'Blessed are the solitary and the elect, for you will find the kingdom, for you came forth from it, and you will return to it again.' Advocacy of solitary existence according to this saying creates contemplative space which results in the discovery of the kingdom. The notion of journey is also important. The seeker of insight will recognize dislocation from place of origin but contemplation is the pathway that allows return to that elevated state. This sense of displacement and pilgrimage is reinforced in the shortest of the sayings in this collection. There Jesus pithily states 'Be passerby' (Saying 42). Physical itinerancy may not be the aim of this saying. Rather, it appears to promote an inner recognition of a lack of place as one seeks a return to the true state of origin and existence. In effect, a sense of disengagement from the world is seen as an essential part of the seeker's spiritual journey. Such a perspective coheres with sayings found in the four canonical gospels: 'the Son of Man has nowhere to lay his head' (Matt. 8.20/Luke 9.58); disciples of Jesus are not to worry about clothing, but rather must learn from the way God adorns the lilies of the field (Matt. 6.28); and the cares of the world 'choke' true discipleship (Mark 4.19).

One particularly interesting aspect of the outlook of the *Gospel of Thomas* is its attitude to various disciples and group leadership. From the outset it is clearly stated that Thomas is the medium through whom the sayings of Jesus are transmitted. This provides Thomas with a certain authoritative function as interpreter of the Jesus tradition. However, in Saying 12, when the disciples enquire directly who will be their leader after Jesus 'departs' from them, it is not Thomas who is designated for this role, but James the Just. This James was the brother of Jesus (Matt. 13.55), who had according to tradition experienced a vision of the risen Jesus (1 Cor. 15.7), and became leader of the church in Jerusalem (Gal. 1.19; 2.9; Acts 12.17). He was put to death by stoning at the behest of Annas the Jewish high priest around AD 61, during the power-vacuum that followed the death while in office of the Roman procurator Festus and prior to the arrival of his successor Albinus. Perhaps more significant than these biographical details is the fact that James is usually seen as representing a form of Jewish Christianity that maintained a more positive attitude towards Jewish law, traditions, and practices. While proclaiming allegiance to Jesus as Messiah, this form of Christianity was in many ways dissonant with the more radical pro-Gentile form of Christianity spread around the eastern Mediterranean and beyond by Paul. It is interesting that the *Gospel of Thomas* promotes the authority of James and thereby aligns itself with some form of Jewish Christianity. Perhaps, however, the link with James the Just in the *Gospel of Thomas* is more a strategy than a theological statement. It is striking that while many of the sayings in *Thomas* are anti-hierarchical and advocate a solitary spirituality, at this point the text draws upon the authority of an individual figure. The issue here may be more to do with legitimating the type of spirituality that is being advocated, by linking the community and its teachings with the heritage of James.

Yet in the saying that follows on from this statement concerning James the Just, Thomas is elevated above two other prominent disciples because of his insight into Jesus' true nature. The purpose of this short narrative is focused upon the correct way to describe Jesus. Moreover, it appears intentionally to correct the confession, which according to Matthew's gospel was made at Caesarea Philippi by Simon Peter. There Peter declared of Jesus that 'you are the Christ, the Son of the living God'. This perspective is affirmed by Jesus, who declares, 'blessed are you, Simon Barjona, for flesh and blood has not revealed this to you, but my Father who is in heaven' (Matt. 16.16–17). By comparison, the *Gospel of Thomas* appears to subvert this perspective with the following exchange between Jesus and three of his disciples, Peter, Matthew, and Thomas:

[1]Jesus said to his disciples, 'Compare me, tell me whom I am like?'
[2]Simon Peter said to him, 'You are like a righteous angel.'
[3]Matthew said to him, 'You are like a wise philosopher.'

⁴Thomas said to him, 'Master, my mouth is wholly incapable of saying whom you are like.'

⁵Jesus said: 'I am not your master. After you drank, and become intoxicated from the bubbling spring which I have measured out.'

⁶And he took him and withdrew. He spoke to him three words.

⁷Then when Thomas returned to his companions, they asked him, 'What did Jesus say to you?'

⁸Thomas said to them, 'If I tell you one of the words which he said to me, you will take up stones and throw them at me; and a fire will come out of the stones and burn you up.'

(Saying 13)

The opening question recalls the twin enquiries made by Jesus at Caesarea Philippi, 'Who do people say the Son of Man is? . . . but who do you say I am?' (Mark 16.13, 15). The choice of both Simon Peter and Matthew as literary foils, whose perspectives are corrected by the mysterious 'non-answer' of Thomas, can perhaps be explained. First, Peter makes the central declaration concerning Jesus which lies at the heart of early Christology – namely, 'Jesus is the Christ, the Son of the living God'. Such 'certainties' seem discordant with the ineffable and veiled nature of Jesus that is affirmed by the Thomasine community.

It is interesting that in this saying the *Gospel of Thomas* changed Peter's 'confession' about Jesus to a declaration that he is 'a righteous angel'. It is uncertain whether this change is designed to make the Petrine position more susceptible to rebuttal, or whether such a declaration is seen as not being incorrect, but represents the lowest stage in a hierarchy or progression of Christological understandings. Either way, such an 'angelomorphic Christology' is viewed as defective by the author either in its entirety or its extent, and interestingly Jesus chooses not to respond to this answer.

While the first type of response may draw on motifs already found in Jewish apocalyptic texts, the second response offered by

38

Matthew, that Jesus is the sagacious philosopher, aligns more with a certain strand of wisdom tradition. The portrayal of Jesus as the supreme teacher is prominent in Matthew's Gospel (Matt. 23.8), and here *Thomas* may be critiquing what it views as the limited understanding that Jesus is simply the rabbi *par excellence*. Finally *Thomas* speaks out and declares that Jesus is beyond categorization or description. Here there seems to be a concatenation of various Jewish mystical tradition tied up with the Christological perspectives of the Thomasine community. It has been suggested that the three unrepeatable words spoken by Jesus are linked with the divine name Yahweh, which because of its sacredness is not uttered in Jewish tradition. When the divine name is discussed during Moses' encounter with God in the wilderness at the burning bush, God provides an allusive response which is encapsulated but not unpacked in three Hebrew words (אחיח אשר אחיח) 'I am who I am' (Exod. 3.14). It is likely that Jesus has revealed to Thomas that he is the one who bears the divine name – and because of the sacred nature of this name Thomas cannot reveal this to his fellow disciples.

Hence the issues of authority figures and Christology are closely linked in the *Gospel of Thomas*. It appears that differences in understanding the essence and nature of Jesus were demarcation points between Thomasine Christians and other branches of the nascent Jesus movement. One further significant authority figure surfaces in *Thomas* in its final saying. Only here is Mary Magdalene mentioned in the text and her gender is presented by Peter as a barrier to her participation in the benefits of community life. There is possibly a critique of the exclusion of women from authority roles in the emergent orthodox church. The response proposed by the Jesus of the *Gospel of Thomas* may strike readers as being misogynistic by modern standards, especially because of its lack of affirmation of Mary as a female. Instead Jesus offers the possibility of some type of gender transformation. 'Jesus said, "Look, I will lead her that I may make her male, in order that she too may become a living spirit resembling you males. For every

The 'gospels' from Nag Hammadi

39

woman who makes herself male will enter into the kingdom of heaven" ' (Saying 114). This type of gender transformation needs to take account of three contemporary factors:

1) the encratic life of the Thomasine community;
2) perspectives on gender change in other non-canonical texts;
3) Jesus' own apparently gender-transcending being in certain texts.

The solitary life advocated in the *Gospel of Thomas* was seen as the path to ascertaining entrance into the kingdom of heaven.

Therefore, in line with the wider phenomenon of developing Christian monasticism, especially in the Egyptian context of the 3rd and 4th centuries, a harsh life of self-denial is seen as a means of pursuing a more elevated spirituality. Other texts that are found in the Nag Hammadi corpus likewise require devotees to undergo some gender change. For instance, the *Gospel of Philip* sees the adherent's spiritual journey as resulting in the reunification of a being's earthly male part with its now separated angelic female part. This view of salvation is to effect a repair of ruptured beings that now are tainted by gendered fragmented pieces of the full being. Finally, in Saying 114, Jesus appears to speak from beyond the realm of gendered existence since he is able to address Peter and his associates as 'you males'. In this sense, Jesus becomes a mystical example for the Thomasine community of wholeness of being that transcends gendered existence. Moreover, it is by reaching beyond narrow gender categories that one is able to enter the kingdom of heaven – which is the goal of members of this community, although their understanding of the kingdom appears radically different to that of their fellow Christians in other communities.

The *Gospel of Thomas* offers a mystical version of Christianity, that is elitist, self-denying, and focused upon a higher realm of existence. Esoteric knowledge and commitment to the secret interpretations of the community are central to its understanding and are the basis of its allegiance to the teachings of Jesus. While the form of mysticism that is found in the *Gospel of Thomas* is far less complex than the detailed cosmologies and assent-journeys found in other texts generally labelled as 'Gnostic', it is possible to see why *Thomas* was a text that appealed to adherents of these more developed belief systems. The *Gospel of Thomas* defies easy categorization. Some of the material it contains is undoubtedly early and may even occasionally preserve versions of sayings that perhaps pre-date the more developed forms found in the canonical gospels. Also in the case of material unparalleled in the canonical gospels, some of these sayings might preserve material which in some form originated with the historical Jesus. Notwithstanding these facts, as the Coptic 4th-century version of the text is preserved, it represents a text that underwent revision, with the accretion of added traditions, to make it 'live' for the successive generations that treasured, used, and quarried these saying to draw themselves closer to the 'living Jesus' who speaks these enigmatic words.

The *Gospel of Philip*

In comparison with the canonical gospels, the *Gospel of Philip* shares very few points of contact with the traditions contained in those four texts. Its outlook is radically dissimilar. It understands salvation not as rescue from sin, but as the reunification of being. Such a process is possible for initiates only through undergoing the ritual of the 'bridal chamber'. While sexual imagery is prevalent in describing this sacral rite that seeks to reunite male and female parts of being, the text in other sections promotes ascetic practices and sexual continence. Therefore the imagery of sexual union appears to be just that – 'imagery'—and not a reflection of physical practice. This is, however, debated, with some scholars understanding the text as promoting sacred intercourse among group members with the voyeuristic participation of the 'sons of the bridal chamber' as a type of 'sacramental practice' in the group.

The text presents a highly developed, although often unclear, cosmology of the soul's progress to higher realms of existence. Perhaps the continuing value of this text is to allow insight into the diversity that existed in ancient Christianity. It has been observed that the *Gospel of Philip* exhibits close connections with Valentinian perspectives on the human state, the salvific transformation, and the mode of existence after death.

Only one partial copy of the *Gospel of Philip* survives. Like the *Gospel of Thomas*, this text is found in what has become numbered as codex II of the Nag Hammadi collection, and is the third text in that volume following on immediately after *Thomas*. What is noteworthy about this arrangement is that it represents the oldest extant example of two non-canonical gospels being collected together in antiquity. Moreover, unless the arrangement is a totally random compendium of miscellaneous texts (and that is not impossible), then presumably the compiler saw at least some connection or similarity of outlook between these texts. This surviving copy of the *Gospel of Philip* was written around the middle of the 4th century, but presumably it was composed somewhat earlier, and for a variety of linguistic reasons it appears likely to have been originally composed in Greek. While the standard critical edition of this text proposed a date of composition in the second half of the 3rd century, scholarly consensus has settled on a slightly earlier dating in the first half of the 3rd century – with some scholars suggesting an even earlier date in the latter half of the 2nd century.

To modern sensibilities, the *Gospel of Philip* appears to be a loosely connected series of rambling material. It is not the diversity of literary forms – such as parables, aphorisms, invective, sayings of Jesus, and dogmatic statements – that gives this impression (for such a range also exists in the canonical gospels). Rather, it is the disjointed flow of material as the text moves from one unit to the next. Due to this lack of a linked sequence of thought, it has been suggested that the *Gospel of Philip* is an incoherent document formed by an editor who excerpted material from existing texts that had a congenial theological outlook. Others have not been quite so negative in their assessment of the structuring of material in the *Gospel of Philip*. It has been helpfully noted that modern assumptions concerning the 'flow' and structure of a literary text should not be applied uncritically to ancient documents. Meandering and digressive writing styles are to be found in many highly prized ancient documents – works such as the *Sentences of Sextus*, or the Egyptian *Instruction of Ankhsheshonqy* – parallel the chain arrangement of ideas found in the *Gospel of Philip*, and this should not automatically be thought of as a chaotic arrangement. Moreover, in the *Gospel of Philip* such chains of disparate material are often linked by catchwords that aid the transition from one section to the next. The contents of this text are not easily catalogued, due to the rapid jumps between ideas and the different types of material found within small blocks of the text. However, it is possible to give a broad-brush outline of some of the most significant material in the *Gospel of Philip*. In the numbering system in the following table, the first number refers to the page number of the codex and the second to the line number. This is the common referencing system.

Reference	Contents
51.29–52.35	Origin, generation, and existence of humans. 'Hebrew' as a reference for an un-spiritual being.
53.1–55.23	Christ's soteriological work, dualistic nature of physical world, deceptive names, animal sacrifices unnecessary, deceptive role of archons.
55.24–55.36	Mary's virginal conception not through the feminine Holy Spirit.
55.37–57.28	Concealed valuable objects as a metaphor for soul hidden in the body.
57.30–59.6	Christ's polymorphic appearances, union with Christ.

1) a number of themes recur almost like a refrain throughout the text;
2) the writer's point is often less than obvious and the very esoteric metaphors seem to be designed for those already 'in the know';
3) a number of sections describe the actual cultic practices of group members.

When reading the *Gospel of Philip*, three features quickly become apparent:

The bridal chamber

Without doubt, the bridal chamber ritual was one of the central liturgical and sacramental practices for Valentinian Christians. This ritual was closely linked to the understanding of the plight of the soul – the eternal aspect of a being that was now trapped in a binding material form. The bridal chamber appears to have been an actual place where a ceremony of reunification, purification, and dedication to a spiritual marriage took place. There was a belief that the material human form was the result of a rupture of the true spiritual being that led to a gender-based separation of being into two parts: the male aspect that had 'fallen' to earth, and become combined and tainted with physical matter; and the female part that was contained in a being's angel and inhabited a higher cosmic level. The soteriological scheme of the *Gospel of Philip* promised the prospect of repairing this gender-based fracturing. One of the key descriptions of the purpose of the bridal chamber ritual clearly shows that its primary concern was the reunification of the female spiritual part of the being with the entrapped male part.

> If the woman had not separated from the man, she should not die with the man. His separation became the beginning of death. Because of this, Christ came to repair the separation, which was from the beginning, and again unite the two, and to give life to those who died as a result of the separation, and unite them. But the woman is united to her husband in the bridal chamber. Indeed, those who have united in the bridal chamber will no longer be

separated. Thus Eve separated from Adam because it was not in the bridal chamber that she united with him.

(*Gos. Phil.* 70.9-22)

It has been suggested that the *Gospel of Philip* offers two differing sequential patterns of initiation involving the bridal chamber. In the first of these typological descriptions, a comparison of the soul's spiritual journey is based upon the physical progression into the Holy of Holies in the Jerusalem Temple. Describing the three buildings or areas of the temple, the author states, 'baptism is the holy building; redemption is the Holy of the Holy; the Holy of Holies is the bridal chamber' (69.22-25). The second pattern (see 70.34-71.10) also involves a progression of soteriological rituals, but encompasses some additional stages and different language to describe such rites. The stages involved are described as rebirth, anointing, redemption, and the bridal chamber. As the rebirth of Jesus is closely linked with him being 'revealed in the Jordan' (70.34), it appears that this rebirth equates to baptism. This is a lower stage of the initiation process than the anointing. This point is made explicitly in the text when the author declares 'the chrism is superior to baptism, for it is from the word chrism that we have been called Christians, certainly not because of the word baptism' (74.12-15). Leaving aside the dubious etymology employed here, it appears that the author is arguing that adherents to the form of Christianity promoted in the *Gospel of Philip* have experienced a higher level of spiritual participation than those who stop at the basic baptismal ritual.

Bridal chamber theology, although not systematically explained, is the culmination of the sequential initiation process. Redemption may in fact not be a discrete stage, but something than occurs through undergoing the bridal chamber rite. The 'marriage' envisaged is the reunification of the initiate (the male) with his angel (the female). Having undergone this process, the reconstituted being must no longer be involved with physical sexual practices. In a broken passage, it appears that those who undergo this ritual are

46

seen as being divinized in some sense, and consequently are known as 'sons of the bridal chamber' (76.3–5). It is interesting to note that baptism, while not totally disparaged, is seen as only the first phase of Christian initiation. There appears to be an implicit criticism of emergent orthodoxy's position that baptism was the only entrance rite required to become a Christian.

Jesus kisses Mary Magdalene

One aspect of the *Gospel of Philip* that has been unduly sensationalized is the scene where Jesus kisses Mary. This broken passage can be translated into English in the following manner to highlight the gaps in the text:

> And the companion of the […] Mary Magdalene. [… loved] her more than [all] the disciples [and used to] kiss her [often] on her […]. The rest of [the disciples …]. They said to him 'Why do you love her more than all of us?'
>
> *(Gos. Phil. 63.30–64.5)*

Despite these gaps in the manuscript, it is obvious that from the perspective of the text, it describes the privileged role of Mary Magdalene and that she enjoys an obvious degree of intimacy in her relationship with Jesus. However, various reconstructions of the text have tried to make the type of relationship more explicit by sexualizing the level of intimacy and describing the kiss as one that is given on the mouth. Typical among the reconstructions is the following:

> And the consort of [Christ is] Mary Magdalene. [The Lord loved Mary] more than [all] the disciples, and kissed her often on her [mouth]. The others too […] they said to him 'Why do you love her more than all of us?'
>
> *(Gos. Phil. 63.30–64.5)*

Too often this is interpreted by conspiracy theorists or the writers of popular literature as providing a window into Jesus' physical relationship with Mary Magdalene and revealing 'a truth' that the institutionalized church has suppressed. The reality is far less exciting. The practice of exchanging kisses among fellow Christian believers is known from the pages of the New Testament. Paul tells the addressees of his Epistle to the Romans to 'greet one another with a holy kiss' (Rom. 16.16). In the wider culture, kisses were a common way of greeting family members and did not carry the same overtones that have become attached to this practice in a highly sexualized modern society. Since many who followed Jesus became ostracized from their families, like many new religious movements Christian literature presented a fictive kinship whereby the replacement family of believers becomes the authentic locus for the use of signs of familial affection. The second factor that needs to be recognized is that in a number of non-canonical gospels Mary becomes a subversive authority figure for the marginalized groups that read these texts. She is presented as a significant figure because of the quality of her insight and discipleship, thereby critiquing the forms of Christianity that centred upon the more structured and hierarchical leadership of figures such as Peter.

The Jesus tradition in the *Gospel of Philip*

Only occasionally does the *Gospel of Philip* present a saying of Jesus. To be precise, in this long text there are only 17 instances of this phenomenon, and 9 of these are citations or modifications of Jesus' words as already found in the canonical gospels. The remaining 8, which are introduced with typical introductory formulae ('the Lord said', 'the Saviour said', or 'he said'), place enigmatic sayings on the lips of Jesus which resonate with Valentinian theology. A few examples illustrate this tendency. In line with the salvific hopes of this form of Christianity, Jesus addresses his disciples saying 'You who have joined the perfect light with the Holy Spirit, unite the angels with us also, as being the images' (*Gos. Phil.* 58.10–14). Here, the doctrine of reunification with the angelic part of one's being is advocated by Jesus, as is the acknowledgement that the earthly part is just the 'image' of a transcendent reality. A fresh Son of Man statement compares Jesus with a dyer.

> The Lord went into the dye works of Levi. He took seventy-two different colours and threw them into the vat. He took them out all white. And he said, 'Even so has the Son of Man come as a dyer.'
>
> (*Gos. Phil.* 63.29–30)

Interestingly, a related version of this story is to be found in some manuscripts of the *Infancy Gospel of Thomas*. The imagery of the 'dyer' also occurs earlier in the *Gospel of Philip* (61.12–20). God is called a dyer, since he dips things in water to make them become immortal. This seems to be an image that is used to describe baptism, the fact that the mixture of 72 colours is transformed to white may be a further allusion to the purification of baptism.

Another enigmatic saying placed on the lips of Jesus which reflects Valentinian cosmology occurs when the Lord said, 'Blessed is he who is before he came into being. For he who is, has been and shall be' (*Gos. Phil.* 64.10–12). Here the emphasis is on the pre-existence of the true 'Gnostic' believer who has the prospect of existing again in that reunified state.

There are almost certainly no additional independent sayings of Jesus contained in the *Gospel of Philip* which derive from the historical Jesus. As a means of understanding the message of the actual person Jesus who taught in 1st-century Galilee, this apocryphal gospel offers nothing. However, as an insight into how 2nd- and 3rd-century Christians in one section of the Jesus movement understood the foundational figure of their faith, there is much that can be learned.

The 'value' of the *Gospel of Philip* is not easy to assess, for it depends on what is being valued. As mentioned above, as a means of gaining insight into the historical Jesus the text could be classed as worthless. However, other historical insights can be gained from this text, especially concerning the type of Christianity practised by a group with a highly mythical and esoteric understanding of salvation. Such perspectives need to be recognized as historically significant, but their historical value stems from understanding the actual contemporary situation from which they emerged and the form of spirituality they promoted. Moreover, such traditions offer the potential to trace an early phase of the reception of the Jesus tradition amongst one small branch of the larger movement that claimed adherence to his teachings. For those interested in the larger history of Christianity and who wish to hear the voices suppressed by the dominant groups that emerged, the *Gospel of Philip* is an invaluable resource.

The *Gospel of Truth*

Unlike the previous two gospels treated in this section, the third text to be considered is not associated with an individual authority figure, such as Thomas or Philip. The *Gospel of Truth* takes its name from the opening clause of the long introductory sentence that commences this work: 'The gospel of truth is joy for those who have received from the Father of truth the grace of knowing him ...'. Furthermore, Irenaeus in his heresiological work *Adversus Haereses* (3.11.9) knows of a Valentinian work circulating under the title of 'Gospel of Truth'. Unfortunately he does not cite the work or discuss its contents at length, so it is impossible to be certain that these two texts are identical, but the evidence is certainly suggestive. If that is the case, then the *Gospel of Truth* found at Nag Hammadi is likely to have been written between AD 140 (the start of Valentinus' career) and AD 180 (the date of composition of Irenaeus' *Adversus Haereses*). This would mean that the *Gospel of Truth* would be one of the earliest surviving Valentinian texts.

Two copies of this text are found among the Nag Hammadi codices. It is the third work in codex I, and the second work in codex XII. Due to the highly fragmentary nature of that second witness to the text, that copy is used chiefly to corroborate readings found in the more complete form which is treated as the base text for most modern editions. Like the *Gospel of Philip*, the work is seen as Valentinian in character, but it may represent an earlier phase of that school of thought. It has been suggested that this work may have functioned as an introduction to Valentinian thought. The intended audience may have been members of the wider Church who had not previously been exposed to the type of elevated philosophical speculations contained in this elitist branch of Christianity. Furthermore, because of the similarities between the ideas in the *Gospel of Truth* and those fragments of Valentinus' own writings preserved by certain early Christian writers, some have suggested that Valentinus himself was the author of this work. Its stylistic flourishes and less developed theological system lends weight to this suggestion, but while it is an attractive proposal, ultimately it remains unprovable.

The *Gospel of Truth* is perhaps not the kind of text that would usually be classed as a 'gospel'. Jesus does not speak, none of his earthly deeds are recorded, and no additional biographical information is provided. Yet for the author of this text in a very real sense this was 'the gospel' since it clearly set out the good news of the restoration of entrapped beings from 'the fog of error'. Whereas certain other 'Gnostic' texts present a radical disjunction between the supreme God who cannot be tainted by the material realm and the host of lower beings who function as intermediaries with the physical world, such a separation is not as convoluted in the *Gospel of Truth*. Admittedly, the material creation is 'the substitute for truth', but through the Word and the Holy Spirit the Father intervenes in a less distant manner. This treatise on salvation outlines 'the Word that came forth from the pleroma, the one who is in the thought and the mind of the Father' (*Gos. Truth* 16.35–36).

The concept of the 'pleroma' is highly significant in Gnostic thought – although the exact meaning of the term is somewhat of a 'moving target'. In wider Greek literature the basic meaning of the term is that of 'fulness'. However, in Christian texts this concept of 'fulness' has a narrower field of reference. It is something that belongs to the Supreme Deity and represents a spiritual sphere that can be inhabited by the perfect 'Gnostic' disciple at the highest level of upward cosmic ascent. Embryonic ideas about the pleroma can be found within the pages of the New Testament. In the prologue to John's Gospel, which was so influential upon Gnostic thinking, the author declares that 'from his [the Word's] fulness we have all received' (John 1.16). According to Colossians, the fulness dwelt within the Son (Col. 1.19, 2.9), and through the participation of believers in the Son they become partakers of this fulness. Such ideas become vastly expanded and developed in numerous Gnostic texts, where often the pleroma becomes the goal of spiritual journey. In this sense, the pleroma is like a nirvanic state of perfect spiritual consciousness, when the deity is purely contemplated and the distractions of material existence have been totally stripped away.

Thus for the author of the *Gospel of Truth*, since the Word comes forth from this realm, there is the possibility of communication between the perfect spiritual realm and the corrupted earthly existence. Moreover, the Word comes forth from the mind and thought of the Father as the medium of communication and vehicle for restoration. The relationship of the Father to the Son was to become the central question in the Christological controversies of the 3rd and 4th centuries. The so-called Logos (or 'Word') Christology of the 2nd century was a key aspect of Justin's thought. In his *First Apology*, he stated that those who lived in accordance with the Logos (here playing with the double meaning of the term both as a philosophical technical term for rationality and also as a title for Jesus) are the true followers of God. He goes on to stress that in Jesus the Logos has become fully revealed. At this point, the thinking of the 'orthodox' Justin is remarkably close to that found in the *Gospel of Truth*, although the latter offers a more developed cosmology of the relationship of the Word to the

Father. Likewise the Holy Spirit is presented as having an extremely close relationship with the Father. The *Gospel of Truth* can describe the Spirit both as the bosom of the Father (*Gos. Truth* 24.10–11) and also as the tongue within the Father's mouth (*Gos. Truth* 26.35–36). This bodily imagery which sees the mouth as belonging to the Father, the Spirit being the tongue in the mouth, and the Word being uttered forth from that vocal organ describes three tightly related entities. Unsurprisingly, the imagery used to describe the relationship of Father, Word, and Spirit is susceptible to the later charge of modalism – which was seen as defective since it basically confused the three persons of the Trinity by saying that God was not in essence Father, Son, and Holy Spirit – but could choose to appear in one of these modes as either whim or necessity demanded. However, it is anachronistic to judge 2nd-century writers by the standards of 4th-century debates. Instead, what is important is to note how in the *Gospel of Truth* the assumed relationship between Father, Word, and Spirit sits comfortably in the wider thought on this issue in the mid-2nd century.

There is a tendency when discussing Gnostic texts to make the generalized classification that they have a 'docetic' understanding of Jesus. The term 'docetic' describes the view that Jesus' humanity was not real, but simply the way he appeared to those who did not have a true perception of his being. In such texts, the true nature of the divine Logos that inhabits the shell of the human form becomes apparent at some stage during the Passion. The divine being usually leaves the outer shell, since it belongs to a higher realm that cannot be tainted by human suffering, or 'passibility'. While a number of Gnostic texts promulgate such an understanding, the *Gospel of Truth* is not one of these. Rather, it describes and celebrates the way in which the death of Jesus communicates the message of the Father through the medium of the cross.

> For this reason Jesus appeared; he put on that book; he was nailed to a tree; he published the edict of the Father on the cross. O such

great teaching! He draws himself down to death though life eternal clothes him. Having stripped himself of the perishable rags, he put on imperishibility, which no one can possibly take away from him. Having entered the empty spaces of terrors, he passed through those who were stripped naked by oblivion, being knowledge and perfection, proclaiming the things that are in the heart, [...] teach those who will receive teaching.

(Gos. Truth 20.24–21.2)

While some of the images may be unfamiliar (such as 'putting on the book'), the basic understanding would appear remarkably similar to what was later to become the 'orthodox' understanding of the death of Jesus. The reality of the crucifixion is affirmed, and Jesus although dying paradoxically is the one clothed in eternal life. There also appears to be a reflection on the tradition of Christ's descent into hell – 'having entered the empty spaces of terrors' – which was such an important motif in medieval thinking. Furthermore, although incomplete, the text also appears to speak of Jesus making a proclamation of his teaching to those beings that inhabit those regions. Such ideas took on great importance in later non-canonical texts such as the *Gospel of Nicodemus*, in which the Lord releases all the righteous from the power of Hades. They are led forth by Adam, the originator of sin, who is given the sign of the cross on his forehead (and in one of the Latin versions, on the heads of all the saints who accompanied him; Latin A, 8.2). He then leads the company of the righteous into heaven.

Another key point of contact between the thought of Justin Martyr and the *Gospel of Truth* in the area of Christology relates to the Son being the possessor of the Father's name. The *Gospel of Truth* states that the Father was pleased to give his own name to the Son (*Gos. Truth* 40.23–41.3). In effect, this name-sharing denotes the status of the Son as the Father's emissary and reveals the privileged relationship they share. In his *Dialogue* with the interlocutor Trypho, Justin makes the striking claim that 'the name of God himself, which he says was not revealed to Abraham or Jacob, was

Jesus' (*Dial.* 75). Without rehearsing the convoluted exegesis of Old Testament passages that Justin provides to substantiate this claim, what is striking is the similarity and centrality of this idea in the works of two writers who would be cast as representing the diametrically opposed poles of 'orthodoxy' and 'heresy' by later Church figures. In fact, comparison of their thought reveals a high level of correspondence at a number of points.

Both truth and error become animate or personified entities in this text. Thus it is stated that 'error became powerful; it worked on its own matter foolishly, not having known the truth. It set about with a creation, preparing with power and beauty the substitute for the truth' (*Gos. Truth* 17.14–20). Here another key concern of Gnostic theology comes to the fore, the explanation of the disruption of the original higher cosmic order and the origins of the material realm. This area of theology, known as protology, is key in many of these mythological texts. It is assumed that by understanding the cause of the original rupture of the ideal state of existence, the Gnostic disciple may begin to pursue the path of return to that higher state. In essence, soteriological concerns are the central aspect of the majority of Gnostic gospels. Such salvation is usually a personal journey, it is interiorized, involves special knowledge and a return to a pristine state of existence. As these notions became more developed and speculative, the ideas of canonical and non-canonical gospels became more obviously polarized. However, the *Gospel of Truth* suggests that in the earlier phases, Gnostic thought could be viewed as not too distant from the wider stream of philosophical Christianity, most notably as represented by writers such as Justin.

The *Gospel of the Egyptians*

The fourth 'gospel' text to be treated from the Nag Hammadi corpus, the *Gospel of the Egyptians*, survives in two independent versions found as the second text in both codex III and codex IV. From the outset, in order to disambiguate between texts, it needs to be noted that the work known by the same title from the writings of various Church Fathers and for which some excerpts are preserved in the writings of Clement of Alexandria is not the same text as that preserved at Nag Hammadi. Usually it is a great help to textual critics to have two versions of the same text; however, in this case the different versions exacerbate problems of reconstruction. The text in codex III originally comprised of 30 pages, but only 26 have been partially or completely preserved. Codex IV is in a much poorer state. Although 'parts of all its eighty-one inscribed pages have been preserved, the majority of them are extant only in fragmentary form and these fragments were thoroughly mixed up by the time these were put in plexiglass containers'. It may be thought that the existence of the copy in codex III would assist in organizing the fragments. However, the two versions represent independent translations of what was presumably an original Greek text. The two versions differ widely in meaning, word order, and choice of terms employed for the Coptic translation. So even prior to attempting to unravel the meaning of this extremely abstruse text, scholars must first try to piece together its form.

The formal title given at the end of this document is *The Holy Book of the Great Invisible Spirit*. However, at the beginning of the colophon on the last page of this text, the work is described as the 'Egyptian Gospel' – hence the source of the modern title. This connection with Egypt is less than obvious. To suggest an Egyptian origin is one possible inference, but there is little to support this apart from the reference in the colophon and the location of discovery (but this does not make other Nag Hammadi texts specifically 'Egyptian'). The association may have more to do with the central figure of Seth in the narrative, and possible associations that had been drawn between the Seth of the Old Testament and the Egyptian god of the same name.

Whereas both the *Gospel of Philip* and the *Gospel of Truth* are plausibly seen as products of the Valentinian school of thinking, the *Gospel of the Egyptians* is noticeably different in its worldview. Centring on the figure of Seth and the race that emanates from him, this tractate is representative of a branch of Gnostic thought usually designated as Sethianism. In fact, the diversity of theological outlooks found among the Nag Hammadi writings is one of the key reasons that some scholars have expressed disquiet over retaining the label 'Gnosticism'. While the observed diversity is a reality, there are points of contact between Valentinian and Sethian thought which probably make the description 'Gnostic' a useful umbrella term as long as it is recognized that it covers a number of related, but not identical, religious belief systems.

The standard critical edition of the *Gospel of the Egyptians* divides the text into four large units:

1) the origin of the heavenly world (III 40.12–55.16 = IV 50.1–67.1);
2) the origin, preservation, and salvation of the race of Seth (III 55.16–66.8 = IV 67.2–78.10);
3) the hymnic section (III 66.8–67.26 = IV 78.10–80.15);
4) the concluding section dealing with the origin and transmission of the tractate (III 68.1–69.17 = IV 80.15–81 end).

The opening section discusses the nature of the supreme God, from whom emanates a series of lesser divine beings. In rank below the supreme God is a trinity of Father, Mother, and Son (*Gos. Eg.* 40.1–4). The Mother figure also bears the name Barbelo. This figure is a well-known character in Sethian texts, but here, after a series of untranslatable magical words, she is described as being self-originating, she concurs with the supreme God, or the Father of silence, she is virginal and presides over heaven. As beings emanate from each of the successive levels of divine figures the silent Father nods his approval and the pleroma of lights is well pleased.

Another feature of the text which appears bizarre to modern readers is the use of what appear to be nonsense words or letter combinations. At one point, the text reads as follows:

Domedon Doxomedon came forth, the aeon of the aeons, and the throne which is in him, and the powers which surround him, the glories and the incorruptions. The Father of the great light who came forth from the silence, he is the great Doxomedon-aeon, in which the thrice-male child rests. And the throne of his glory was established in it, this one on which his unrevealable name is inscribed, on the tablet [...] one is the word, the Father of the light of everything, he who came forth from the silence, while he rests in the silence, he whose name is in an invisible symbol. A hidden, invisible mystery came forth iiiiiiiiiiiiiiiiii[iii]

ēēēēēēēēēēēēēēēēēē[ēē o]ooooooooooooooooooooo uu[uuu] uuuuuuuuuuuuuuuuuuuu eeeee eeeeeeeeeeeeeeee aaaaaaaa [aaaa] aaaaaaaaaaaa ōōōōōōōōō[ōō] ōōōōōōōōōō.

(Gos. Egyptians 43.8–44.9)

The symbolic significance of these vowels is a mystery. They are somehow related to the divine name. Perhaps they are seen as being the vowels that enable one to sound the divine name YHWH, which since Hebrew is a consonantal alphabet does not contain the required vowels. While the best that can be achieved is informed speculation, such non-standard letter combinations appear in a range of other texts, such as the *Books of Jeu*, and for the devotee of such esoteric knowledge they are often understood as secret passwords that allowed the progress of the soul's upward ascent through cosmic spheres that were guarded and closed to those without such information.

The mythology that is outlined is often beyond the comprehension of modern readers and one suspects that only those 'insiders' fully immersed in the secret meanings of the text would have any chance of grasping the hidden esoteric sense of these recondite writings. The purpose of such texts was to veil their hidden wisdom from outsiders. They have certainly succeeded in this goal.

Conclusions

These four 'gospels' found among the Nag Hammadi corpus of texts show vast differences in the literary forms they employ, the transparency of their contents, and the underlying cosmological systems that govern their worldview. By comparison, the four canonical gospels show a far higher degree of homogeneity in form and theological outlook. Admittedly, the Gospel of John is somewhat different in tone from the other three canonical accounts, but when compared to the range of non-canonical texts considered here the differences among the canonical accounts appear relatively minor.

This raises the larger question of how such a disparate group of texts were brought together in the same collection. We know nothing of the person or group responsible for the collection, but it can be observed that the perspectives of these four Nag Hammadi gospels, although different, do nonetheless have various similarities. They all promote the pursuit of hidden knowledge, they offer hermeneutical keys to progress in the spiritual journey, in various ways they are all world-denying, and their chief concern is soteriological – seeking the salvation of the individual and a return to a repristinated state of being. For elitist mystical Christians, such a diverse range of texts was presumably a repository of spiritual ideas that enriched one's ascent through the heavenly spheres.

Examination of the texts themselves both problematizes and yet simultaneously helps in answering the question, 'what is a gospel?' A text like the *Gospel of Thomas* shows that a series of sayings attributed to Jesus could be regarded by certain disciples as encapsulating the core teachings of the movement's foundational figure. By contrast, in the *Gospel of Philip*, although not totally absent, sayings are minimized, and descriptions of liturgical rites and a compendium of Valentinian beliefs constitute 'a gospel' for those who read this text. The *Gospel of Truth* records no sayings or deeds of the earthly Jesus – yet the text remains very Christocentric.

It stands in a stream of Christological reflection that asserts that Jesus is to be understood as the divine Logos. This understanding, which in its own day was the prevalent means of representing the relationship between the Father and the Son, may suggest that the outlook of the *Gospel of Truth* was perhaps not seen as aberrant in its contemporary setting as it would be viewed by later generations. However, what is striking is that a text written in the form of a treatise with little concern to record the words or deeds of the historical Jesus could nonetheless self-referentially call itself a 'gospel'. Finally, the *Gospel of the Egyptians* is perhaps the text that looks least like what most people would understand as a gospel. In fact, this text may even represent the 'Christianization' of a pre-Christian complex salvation myth. So how does one answer the question, 'what is a gospel?' In part, it depends on the selection of texts that are allowed to be described by that term. The approach here has been to consider texts from Nag Hammadi that refer to themselves as gospels or have the word 'gospel' appended to them as titles or colophons. Admittedly, this may cast a wide net – but it is representative of the usage of the term in early Christian circles.

Chapter 3
The infancy gospels

The infancy of Jesus in the canonical accounts

In the earliest surviving Christian writings – the letters of
Paul – there is little interest in the events surrounding the early
life of Jesus. Indeed, for Paul, only two 'facts' from that phase of
Jesus' life seem to have been of importance, because of their
theological significance. First, Jesus was a descendant of David
(Rom. 1.4) and secondly, he was born of a woman (Gal. 4.4). If
these fleeting details could not have been exploited for theological
purposes it is virtually certain that Paul would not have alluded to
them. Similarly, the earliest canonical gospel – Mark – opens with
Jesus commencing his public ministry in Galilee. However, the
curiosity of early believers naturally meant they wanted to know
more and more about the life and origins of Jesus. The author of
John's Gospel described Jesus' origins in a brilliantly cosmological
way, which equated Jesus with the Logos that featured in the
Jewish wisdom tradition. Such a theological innovation provided
some of the major impetus for the more developed cosmologies
found in other early Christian texts, such as those discovered at
Nag Hammadi. However, that approach was not the only
possibility.

Among the canonical evangelists, Matthew and Luke both relate
events from the earthly life of Jesus prior to his public ministry.

These 'hidden years' have intrigued and fascinated believers down through the centuries, and the very compressed details contained in Matthew and Luke represent the beginning of a process of 'reconstructing' the early life of Jesus that increased in late antiquity, flourished in the medieval period, and has continued even in the works of modern authors. In his opening two chapters, Matthew combines purported historical details with theological interpretation. Above all, Jesus' Davidic pedigree is affirmed. He is presented as belonging to the kingly line and is described as being born at home in Bethlehem, the city of David (Matt. 2.7–11). When his father Joseph (who is the second biblical seer of dreams by the name of Joseph, cf. Gen. 37.39–50) is warned in a dream the family have an exodus *into* Egypt prior to returning to Nazareth, a city of Galilee, after the death of Herod the Great.

Luke's account shares many details in common with Matthew, but there are also striking differences. Mary, not Joseph, receives angelic visions. The hometown is Nazareth, not Bethlehem. Yet nonetheless, the couple travel to Bethlehem because of a census that requires people to be enrolled in their ancestral homes. Jesus is not born at home, but at an inn. And contrary to Matthew, there are no magi (wise men) who present gifts, but simple shepherds who come to observe the newborn child.

Both stories do identify the parents – named as Joseph and Mary – the actual birth takes place in Bethlehem, and there is an association with Nazareth. These narratives reveal a core of shared traditions, but they create decidedly different ways of weaving these details into an extended narrative. Luke alone, among the canonical gospels, records an incident from the adolescent years – the family visit to Jerusalem when Jesus is 12 years old (Luke 2.41–52). During this visit, the family unwittingly leave the prodigious youngster behind in the city where, in common with childhood stories of prominent figures in antiquity, he already displays his phenomenal abilities by demonstrating a wisdom that surpasses his years. Such scant details of the 'hidden years' perhaps created more interest than satisfying readers' curiosity. Later writers sought to please pious readers by supplying additional information. It may be debated whether the non-canonical accounts of the young Jesus represent mere fabrications or enshrine kernels of historical incidents. However, it is apparent that in order to make an informed answer, it is necessary to consider those non-canonical traditions in some detail.

The *Infancy Gospel of Thomas*

One of the better known non-canonical texts, the *Infancy Gospel of Thomas* contains some of the most striking and bizarre of Jesus' miracles. Yet these are challenging not only because of their intrinsic implausibility. The greater challenge arises from the portrait they create of the child Jesus. No model Victorian child Jesus here, whom the hymn writer could laud as 'meek and mild'. Instead readers are confronted with a precocious and capricious child, 'shaming teachers and maiming playmates', who constantly leaves a trail of havoc wherever he goes – and this is presumably from the pen of a scribe who wrote as a pious follower of Jesus. No wonder such a portrait of the uncontrollable *enfant terrible* has left subsequent readers bemused concerning the purpose of this text.

This gospel account covers a period of approximately 7 years of Jesus' life. It opens, after the initial prologue, by recounting a story that occurred when Jesus was 5 years old and it concludes by telling its own modified version of the story recorded in Luke's Gospel of the visit of the 12-year-old Jesus and his family to Jerusalem. The text of the *Infancy Gospel of Thomas* was known in antiquity. However, the title attached to it was either simply the 'Gospel of Thomas' (mentioned by Origen, Hippolytus, and others) or the 'Childhood of Jesus' (mentioned by John Chrysostom, Epiphanius of Salamis, and others). Among modern scholars, the confusion that the first title caused with the sayings *Gospel of Thomas* was not appreciated until fragments of the latter text were discovered in the late 19th century. Thus comments of early

Christian writers to the effect that the *Gospel of Thomas* was a 'Gnostic' text led scholars working on the *Infancy Gospel of Thomas* to misunderstand the character of the text. This initial problem has been clarified, but many others remain.

Most notably, the form – or maybe forms – of the text require further clarification. A manuscript (subsequently lost) of the *Infancy Gospel of Thomas* was first described, briefly, in a modern scholarly work in a catalogue of 1675. A second manuscript was then published by J. B. Cotelier in his 1698 edition of the *Apostolic Constitutions*, but this was a fragmentary version of the text. Over the next 150 years, further manuscripts of the text were found. The colossus of 19th-century textual criticism, Constantin von Tischendorf, published in 1853 what has become the standard scholarly edition of the text. He actually published two versions of the text. The first, based primarily on two 15th-century manuscripts and known as Greek A, presented a 19-chapter version of the text. Today this represents the better-known form of the text. Alongside this he published a shorter form, Greek B, based on a manuscript he found during his visit to St Catherine's monastery in the Sinai. He also drew attention to several Latin witnesses to the text. These demonstrate the wide circulation and popular appeal of the narrative. Since Tischendorf's day, the body of manuscripts of the text has increased, with at least 11 extant Greek manuscripts now known. Most significantly, in 1927 Delatte published a 15th-century manuscript which, while closer to the form of Greek A than Greek B, showed greatest affinities with the Latin witnesses and was seen as a witness to another textual form labelled as Greek D. Further discoveries have demonstrated that this text was translated into languages other than Latin, including Syriac, Georgian, Ethiopic, Slavonic, and Irish. The *Infancy Gospel of Thomas* certainly has not been a 'hidden text' down through the centuries.

The prologue to the text opens with a self-attribution of authorship to a 'Thomas, the Israelite' and presents itself as sharing details of Jesus' childhood with non-Jewish believers.

I, Thomas the Israelite, am reporting to you, all my non-Jewish
brothers and sisters, to make known the extraordinary childhood
deeds of our Lord Jesus Christ – what he did after his birth in my
region. This is how it all started:

(Inf. Gos. Thom. 1.1)

After this brief description of author and purpose, this racy
narrative rapidly moves on to relating the spectacular and at times
lurid miracles of the boy Jesus.

The first is innocuous enough. At the age of 5, Jesus fashions
12 clay sparrows beside a flowing stream, and as part of this
process he makes ponds of water from the stream and then
instantly purifies the water with 'a single word'. This innocent
narrative then introduces a dark side which both foreshadows
later confrontations in Jesus' life and at the same time
stigmatizes Jewish attitudes to the law. The narrator notes that
Jesus' actions took place on the Sabbath and that what he had
done was observed by a Jew. This unnamed figure calls Joseph,
the father of Jesus, and informs him that his son 'has violated
the Sabbath'. Joseph joins in haranguing his son for this
Sabbath transgression. Jesus does not address the two adults,
but instead speaks to the clay sparrows: 'Be off, fly away, and
remember, you who are now alive.' The compliant birds do as
they are instructed, and although amazed the Jews (now
plural) report these happening to their leaders.

Three features which are common to many later Christian texts
are immediately apparent. First, the miraculous elements of the
Jesus tradition are heightened. In a pre-Enlightenment age, a
more miraculous Jesus was seen as being able to attract more
followers. The story perhaps was not understood as straining
credulity, but rather as a way of commending faith. Second,
anti-Jewish sentiments are also increased and there is a greater
divide between 'Jews' and Jesus, to whom that label is not
applied. It is noteworthy that at this stage in the story Joseph is

8. The infancy gospels had widespread impact on popular piety and artistic representations of scenes from the life of Christ. Here, drawing upon the *Infancy Gospel of Thomas*, the boy Jesus brings to life clay he had fashioned on the Sabbath

an ambiguous character, who although siding with the Jewish informer is not labelled as a Jew himself. The text should be classified as anti-Jewish rather than anti-Semitic since it appears that there is no racial or ethnic prejudice against Semitic people as a whole. Rather, the Jews, who are viewed as a religious grouping opposed to the claims of Jesus' messiahship, are seen as recalcitrant and deserve whatever judgments are visited upon them. Third, it should be observed that while the category 'Jewish' is viewed negatively, the notion of being an 'Israelite' is taken over as a way of identifying the putative author of this text. There is, therefore, an implicit 'supersessionary' theology at work whereby Christians see themselves as inheritors of the covenantal promises made to the nation of Israel, but conveniently deny any link between historic Israel and the contemporary Jewish people.

The next two stories take a macabre turn. Following the narrative of the story about the vivified clay sparrows, a young boy named as the 'son of Annas the scholar' drains the pools of water that were made by Jesus. An enraged Jesus responds with bitter invective, 'Sodomite, ungodly and ignorant. What harm did the pools of water do to you? From this moment you too will dry up like a tree, and you will never produce leaves or root or bear fruit' (*Inf. Gos. Thom.* 3.2). In response to this curse, the boy withers up and dies.

Next in this episodic drama, while Jesus is going through his village another boy running along innocently bumps him on the shoulder. For the second time the petulant Jesus is angered. He shouts, 'You will not continue your journey', and another child drops dead. The people of the village and the parents of this dead boy speak in similar confused and fearful tones:

> Some people saw what had happened and said, 'Where has this boy come from? Everything he says happens instantly!' The parents of the dead boy came to Joseph and blamed him saying, 'Because you have such a boy, you cannot live with us in the village, or else teach him to bless and not curse. He is killing our children!'
>
> (*Inf. Gos. Thom.* 4.3–4)

There is no doubt that the stories are fascinating, but what motivated the creation of narratives that portray the young Jesus as insolent, uncontrolled, and murderous? Later in the *Infancy Gospel of Thomas* Jesus' behaviour is transformed from that of being a life-taker to that of a life-restorer. Perhaps the message stems from this reversal in Jesus' character. It may be intended to encourage the reversal of uncontrolled behaviour in other people, but it would appear unusual to present Jesus as a character who was in need of personal reform. Chapter 5 of the text offers a slightly different perspective through a dialogue between the boy Jesus and his father Joseph. In response to questioning, Jesus declares that the words he has spoken are not his own and also that the people must take their punishment. When an exasperated

Joseph grabs the ear of Jesus, the child responds 'It is one thing for you to seek and not find; it is quite another for you to act this unwisely. Do you not know that I do not really belong to you? Do not make me upset' (*Inf. Gos. Thom.* 5.5–6). From the perspective of the narrative, the stories seem more concerned to reveal something about the hidden identity of Jesus. The stories are somewhat reminiscent of Old Testament stories where people die for infringing the holiness of God. In particular, there is an incident when a certain man called Uzzah touched the Ark of the Covenant when he thinks it is about to topple off the cart on which it is being transported. His punishment is that 'God struck him down there for his irreverence' (2 Sam. 6.7). The *Infancy Gospel of Thomas* may want readers to identify the boy Jesus with the holiness of the God of the Old Testament.

Choice of school is often a hard decision, and at the best of times teacher–pupil relations can be strained. With such a dangerous and petulant child, the problems, as the narrative now makes clear, become even more unpredictable. There are three scenes that depict the schooling of Jesus. The first is an extended story in the narrative when an unfortunate school master by the name of Zacchaeus mistakenly believes he can both teach and discipline the child (*Inf. Gos. Thom.* 6.1–8.4). When Zacchaeus attempts to teach Jesus letters, the child launches forth on the mystical meaning of each letter. Here the text shows its closest point of contact with the esoteric learning of mystery cults or Gnostic forms of religion. However, these similarities are slight and their purpose is to show the superiority of Jesus' learning, not to promote Gnostic forms of Christianity. Perplexed, the confused Zacchaeus makes a number of insightful comments about Jesus. He states, 'this child is no ordinary mortal ... perhaps he was born before the creation of the world'. Later he goes on to say, 'what great thing he is – god or angel or whatever else I might call him – I do not know' (*Inf. Gos. Thom.* 7.4, 11). The type of faith being offered to readers is highly miracles-based. The wonder-working Jesus is the one in whom followers should place their trust.

On two other occasions there are attempts to school Jesus. The story in chapter 14 is really a doublet and shorter version of the early story. Jesus is unresponsive to the instruction to write out the alphabet. After a period of silence, he challenges the unnamed school master to explain the meaning of the letters. The exasperated teacher strikes Jesus and as a result is cursed and left unconscious (*Inf. Gos. Thom.* 14). The third time Joseph agrees to Jesus attending school, the new school master recognizes that Jesus already possesses more knowledge than he himself does. Adopting a more deferential attitude, this third teacher gains an irenic response from Jesus. This results in a promise to heal the second teacher, who had been struck down because of his confrontation with Jesus earlier in the narrative (*Inf. Gos. Thom.* 15.7). It is interesting that the tradition about Jesus learning letters and then displaying superior esoteric knowledge of their intrinsic meaning is known outside of the *Infancy Gospel of Thomas* (Irenaeus, *Adversus Haereses* 1.20.1). Thus a variant of the story, which is closer to the shorter form contained in *Inf. Gos. Thom.* 14, was in circulation at least by the second half of the 2nd century. This does not demonstrate that the *Infancy Gospel of Thomas* was composed by this time, since it may have incorporated this tradition into its text, but it does show that such stories of Jesus' childhood were already of interest to certain Christians by this stage.

Jesus' hyperactive behaviour does not always result in acts that terrorize those around him. Admittedly from mixed motives, in chapter 9 Jesus raises a child who had fallen from a roof and died. This occurs after the dead boy and other children including Jesus were playing on the roof. Since the other playmates have run away, in order to defend himself against the accusation that he pushed the child from the roof, Jesus brings the boy back to life so he may witness to his innocence. In chapter 10, Jesus miraculously heals a young man who has died of blood loss after cutting his foot with an axe. Next, when a water pitcher accidentally breaks, Jesus carries water home in his cloak (*Inf. Gos. Thom.* 11). Jesus causes super-abundant harvests (*Inf. Gos. Thom.* 12); makes short planks of wood extend to help his father (*Inf. Gos. Thom.* 13); saves James, the son of his father – interestingly not described as Jesus' brother – from a viper bite (*Inf. Gos. Thom.* 16); runs to the aid of an infant who has died and brings him back to life (*Inf. Gos. Thom.* 17); and returns to life a man who falls to his death on a construction site (*Inf. Gos. Thom.* 18).

There is little doubt that the longer form of the text (Greek A) presents a positive progression and development in the behaviour of Jesus. His behaviour as one who maims and murders is transformed as he becomes a healer and restorer of life. However, it has recently been suggested that the shorter form (Greek B) is closer to the original form of the text. Stories contained in chapters 10, 17, and 18 are thus seen as attempts to ameliorate the unpalatable portrait of Jesus as he changes from one who curses to one who blesses. If the shorter form is indeed original, then the text presents a cursing wonder-worker and maintains this characterization more uniformly throughout the narrative. It is not totally obvious why this would have been an attractive understanding of the boy Jesus. Perhaps this develops a Christology of Jesus as judge. This proposal is supported by the observation that in chapter 5 Jesus sees it as his role to mete out 'punishment' on the inhabitants of the village.

The text of the *Infancy Gospel of Thomas* ends by narrating a revised form of the story of the visit to Jerusalem (Luke 2.42–51). This provides strong evidence for seeing the text as post-Lukan, and therefore as being written no earlier than the 2nd century. Many details are embroidered in such a way as to emphasize the astounding wisdom of Jesus. In the *Infancy Gospel of Thomas* Jesus is not only 'sitting among the teachers, listening to them and asking them questions' (Luke 2.46), but is more actively engaged in legal debate, and there is greater detail provided about the nature of the material under discussion.

After three days they found him in the temple area, sitting among
the teachers, listening to the law and asking them questions. All eyes
were on him, and everyone was astounded that he, a mere child,
could interrogate the elders and teachers of the people and explain
the main points of the law and the parables of the prophets.

(Inf. Gos. Thom. 19.4–5)

This expansion of the Lukan description more emphatically
presents Jesus as an authoritative teacher and as a Torah expert.
The other striking feature about this final chapter is that here
for the first time Mary is explicitly introduced into the narrative. In
contrast to the negative representation of Joseph, Mary is
presented in a positive way and receives the veneration of the
Pharisees through the blessing they address to her. Here is the
most obvious place where the pious veneration of emerging 2nd-
century Mariology replaces the more negative aspects of the
biblical text. At this juncture in Luke (2.50), it is stated that the
parents 'did not understand what he [Jesus] was talking about'.
This is replaced by the beatitude addressed to Mary, which draws
upon the doxology uttered to Mary by Elizabeth in chapter 1 of
Luke's account. Thus she is told, 'You are first among women
because God has blessed the fruit of your womb, for we have never
seen or heard of such glory and such virtue and wisdom' *(Inf. Gos.
Thom.* 19.10).

The *Infancy Gospel of Thomas* radically expands and supplements
the one story known about Jesus from the canonical accounts
during the period after his infancy until the start of his public
ministry. Covering the years in Jesus' life between the ages of 5 and
12, the text creates a storyline that is rich in folkloric details,
resulting in a narrative that is both fantastic and fanciful. To assess
the value of the text in historical terms concerning the actual
events it describes will obviously result in a particularly low
estimate of its worth. However, the text is valuable not for
revealing facts about the life of Jesus, but for providing a more
complete picture of one of the various ways that Christians of the

2nd and 3rd centuries expanded the Jesus story in line with their own pious beliefs and theological concerns. While the *Infancy Gospel of Thomas* is an entertaining text, it is also definitely theologically challenging. There are no easy or obvious answers to the question concerning what motivated an author to present the young Jesus in such an uncongenial manner, at least to modern ears. The longer recension accommodates the problem by showing development in the character of Jesus; the shorter (and perhaps earlier) form makes few attempts to solve such problems. In that textual version the young Jesus is a figure of cursing and judgment.

The *Protevangelium of James*

The problems of defining the term 'gospel' in relation to a literary genre have already been highlighted both by general discussion and through consideration of specific texts that have had that label applied to them. Since a large amount of the material in the *Protevangelium* pertains to events prior to the birth of Jesus, it is correct to ask whether this text should be classified as a gospel. Although the usual title of this work contains the Latinized word -*evangelium* meaning 'gospel', not only is this qualified by the prefix *proto-*, showing that the events are prior to the usual starting point of the gospel story, but even more importantly it should be recognized that the title *Protevangelium of James* is in fact a modern construct and not actually the title provided by the text.

Like so many ancient books, the title of this work is not found at the beginning, but at the end. In the final verse of the brief epilogue, the twin-title 'Birth of Mary, Revelation of James' is supplied. While these twin ancient titles may be preferable to the modern construct of *Protevangelium of James*, these are not without their own problems. In comparison with other ancient texts labelled as 'Revelations' or 'Apocalypses', this writing is devoid of much of the apocalyptic imagery that is a feature of that literary genre. The description 'Birth of Mary' is perhaps more useful, but this text is far more than a simple birth-story of Mary, since it tells of events down to the early years of Mary's own mother. So one is left with the conventional title, the *Protevangelium of James*, as the accepted way to describe this text.

It is sometimes suggested that a fundamental difference between canonical and non-canonical gospels is that whereas the former enjoyed widespread circulation throughout the early Church, the latter were read only in small isolationist conventicles that were themselves representative of aberrant forms of Christianity. Not only is such an understanding historically anachronistic, retrojecting the 4th-century structure of a dominant orthodoxy into the 2nd century, when there were multiple expressions of Christianity struggling to define beliefs, but it is just plain wrong in representing the use of at least some of the non-canonical gospels as being highly limited. The *Protevangelium of James* was a particularly widely read document in many branches of Christianity. Based on the evidence of surviving manuscripts, the wide circulation of this document is amply attested. To date, more than 140 Greek manuscripts have been catalogued. The text is also witnessed in numerous translational versions, including Sahidic, Coptic, Syriac, Armenian, Georgian, Ethiopic, Slavonic, and Arabic. In fact, the Arabic text may have influenced Qur'anic and later Islamic understandings of the place of Mary in the Christian tradition.

The lack of a complete surviving Latin manuscript may initially seem odd, but a number of factors account for this. It is almost certain that the *Protevangelium of James* did exist at some stage in Latin translation. Some Latin fragments of similar traditions have been identified as the remains of a manuscript of this text (although this is contested), but more importantly the fact that it was known to the compiler of the Gelasian Decree also strongly suggests the existence of a Latin version. The Decree, written no earlier than the 5th century, contains lists of accepted and rejected writings, among which is listed in the apocryphal category, and hence to be rejected, a work described as the 'book of the nativity of the saviour and of Mary or the midwife'. This description aligns closely with the contents of the *Protevangelium of James*, and consequently there is good reason to suspect the same text is being described.

Given the probable existence of this text in Latin, its disappearance can be attributed to two factors. First, much of its content seems to have been absorbed into larger expanded versions of infancy and childhood compilations of stories such as *The Gospel of Pseudo-Matthew*, *The Life of Joseph the Carpenter*, and *The Gospel of the Birth of Mary*. Yet a more fundamental reason for the loss of the Latin textual tradition was because in the Western Church the text was deemed to be suspect because of its teaching about Joseph's first marriage. As certain sections of the Church became fixated on virginity as a spiritual discipline and a purer state of being, not only was it necessary to present Mary as a perpetual virgin – a key concern of the *Protevangelium* – but the perpetual virginity of Joseph was also asserted. Since the storyline of the *Protevangelium* presented Joseph as an elderly widower with surviving children, this text became highly problematic in the Latin Church. However, within the orthodox tradition the perpetual virginity of Joseph did not feature as a doctrinal concern. Consequently, the text circulated widely and shaped orthodox beliefs, as is attested by the wealth of surviving manuscripts.

Outline of the text

The text, in its current form, can be divided into three major sections which refer to separate though related phases in the life of Mary, together with a brief epilogue giving details of the pseudonymous author.

SECTION	OVERVIEW OF CONTENTS
1.1–8.2	Mary's conception, birth, and events until her adolescence.
8.3–16.8	'Marriage' to Joseph, pregnancy, and preservation of virginity.
17.1–24.14	Journey to Bethlehem, birth of Jesus, violent events.
25.1–4	Epilogue: putative author and circumstances of composition.

It is only in the third section that the text overlaps with the versions of the nativity and infancy stories found in the gospels of Matthew and Luke. The material in the first two sections of the *Protevangelium of James* is a mix of legendary details and pious theologizing. There is little in this text that can be seen as describing historically the actual events it purports to report. Instead its historical value arises from the way it provides a reflection of the religious and social context which enabled such a text to be written, read, and circulated. Its concerns surrounding the cult of virginity, the attitude that incredible miracles commended rather than hindered belief, and the devotion to Mary are all in accord with the wider tastes of many Christians from the late 2nd century onwards.

Section 1: *Prot. Jas.* 1.1–8.2

Within the opening section, there is a description of Mary's conception, birth, and significant life events until her adolescence. The devices used to 'prove' that Mary had not been tainted by the impurity of her parents' sexual union stand very much at the foreground of the concerns of this text. While similar perspectives are present in the canonical stories of the birth of Jesus, the degree of elaboration and intricacy is much less pronounced in the accounts written by Matthew and Luke. Obviously by the time the *Protevangelium* was written, there was a much greater interest in

9. Marian piety resulted in scenes from Mary's childhood as related in the *Protoevangelium of James* being depicted in art. This example is by Albrecht Dürer, *Presentation of the Virgin in the Temple* (1502–3)

the virginal state. One striking feature of the opening section is the way the narrative is based on Old Testament stories of barren couples miraculously conceiving. The two most famous examples are the story of Abraham and Sarah's conception of Isaac, and the birth of the prophet Samuel to his barren mother Hannah. While elements of the Abraham–Sarah story can be detected in the *Protevangelium*, without doubt it is the story of Hannah conceiving Samuel that shapes the legend of the birth of Mary.

To recap that story (1 Sam. 1–2), the barren Hannah is married to Elkanah, who also has another wife, Peninnah, who has borne him many children. Peninnah is described as Hannah's rival. During the annual family pilgrimage to the temple-shrine in Shiloh, the priest Eli promises that her prayer for a child will be answered. The promise comes to fruition, and after the boy Samuel is weaned, Hannah deposits him in the temple in accordance with her vow. Hannah sings a song of praise to the Lord as an outpouring of her sense of blessing. Samuel becomes a figure of purity in the Shiloh temple, contrasting with the venial behaviour of Eli's own sons.

When compared with this story, the similarities of the *Protevangelium* become immediately apparent. The name of the barren woman who will give birth to Mary is Anna. In Greek there is no 'h' sound, so when the story of 1 Samuel is translated into the Greek version of the Old Testament known as the Septuagint, the Hebrew name Hannah is written as Ἄννα 'Anna'. Both women are barren; where Hannah is tormented by Elkanah's other wife, Anna is mocked by her servant Juthine. This may be a detail which is also related to the way that Sarah is mocked by her maidservant Hagar. Anna sings two songs in the opening section. The first is a lament, totally different in tone to Hannah's joyful song. Yet later Anna sings her second song in the narrative, no longer of mourning but an outpouring of praise. Here is the more direct parallel to the song of Hannah contained in 1 Samuel 2, and simultaneously the counterpoint to Anna's own earlier lament (*Prot. Jas.* 3.2–8). There is little doubt that the author of the *Protevangelium*, in light of the absence of historical source material for the birth of Mary, chose to give his narrative a biblical flavour by basing it on the story of Samuel's birth.

The text of the *Protevangelium* commences with a description of Anna's husband, Joachim, an Israelite, whose piety and prosperity are exemplified by his gift offerings to the Lord. On an unspecified festival day, Joachim is prevented from presenting his offering first by a slightly officious individual called Reubel. Aside from his name, nothing is known of Reubel apart from his protest, 'you are not allowed to offer your gifts first because you have not produced an Israelite child' (*Prot. Jas.* 1.5). Joachim consults a work or record known as *The Twelve Tribes of the People* and discovers that all the righteous members of Israel indeed produced offspring. From frustration and bewilderment he retires to the desert, fasting 'forty days and forty nights', and determines 'not to go back to food or drink until the Lord my God appears to me' (*Prot. Jas.* 1.11). This creates tension in the narrative, with readers wondering how such an ultimatum will be resolved. However, at virtually the same point in the story as Anna receives an angelic visitation telling her she will conceive, she is also informed that her husband has received a similar vision and is returning home. The text is surprisingly restrained at this point in reporting Joachim's vision second-hand, rather than giving a dramatic account of the events as they supposedly transpired. During this angelic report to Anna of the vision seen by her husband, the actual words spoken to Joachim are recounted.

Here there is a fascinating textual problem. Some manuscripts read 'behold your wife Anna has conceived in the womb', while others state, 'behold your wife Anna will conceive in the womb'. If the future tense were to be preferred, then the note in 4.10 that 'Joachim rested the first day at home' could be read euphemistically as the time when the predictive promise was brought to fruition. The textual evidence, however, appears to favour the perfect tense, since the earlier Greek manuscripts contain this reading. This would then imply that Anna was already pregnant, miraculously, by the time Joachim arrived home. Such a reading would align with the piety of this document which goes to extraordinary lengths to affirm Mary's purity. It would be strange if its author had allowed the heroine of his story to be tainted with carnal concupiscence. Hence, in this text it is possible to see the emergence of a theology of the immaculate conception of Mary, although it is not framed in such theologically developed terms.

Folkloric elements punctuate the remainder of the first section after Anna gives birth to Mary. The text recounts the lengths to which Anna goes to preserve ritual purity for Mary. This includes not allowing her to walk on common ground (6.3), transforming the girl's bedroom into a sanctuary (6.4), and engaging 'undefiled' Hebrew females to entertain the infant Mary. Such tropes are not uncommon in the legends of the childhood years of sacred figures. The act of handing Mary over to the temple is reported in a highly liturgical fashion with processions and acts of devotion to the young girl. Undefiled Hebrew women are summoned to form a lamp-lit procession accompanying Mary so her heart will not be 'captivated by things outside the temple' (7.5). The priest kisses and blesses Mary on her arrival (7.7). She is sat on the third step of the altar, she dances in the temple and is the darling of the people of Israel (7.9–10). She is fed directly from the hand of an angel (8.2). Such characterization presents Mary in a manner that approaches that of a goddess being venerated in her own sacred shrine. Yet this situation of blissful veneration of childhood innocence is problematized as Mary approaches her adolescence.

Section 2: *Prot. Jas.* 8.3–16.8

The narrative sets up another tension to progress the storyline. Governed by the Levitical laws, the priests in the temple are aware that with Mary approaching puberty her menstrual flows will defile the sanctuary (this is based on stipulations in the Old Testament, Lev. 12.1–6; 18.19). Fortunately, in this text angels are ever present to help out pious humans confronted by tricky religious conundrums! The angel informs the high priest that he is to assemble the widowers of the people and Mary will be married off to whichever one is identified with a miraculous sign. Among the assembled widowers is Joseph. Presumably the choice of widowers is meant to signal to readers that the men in question are beyond the stage of sexual desire. A dove lands on Joseph's head and this is taken as being the promised divine sign. Joseph attempts to resist this choice. Theologically, it is interesting that one of the reasons he puts forward to demonstrate why he is unsuitable for the role is 'I already have sons and I am an old man' (*Prot. Jas.* 9.8). Thus, the *Protevangelium* can be seen to support in condensed form what became known as the Epiphanian solution to the problem of accounting for the siblings of Jesus.

In the New Testament (Mark 6.3; Matt. 13.55–56), there are instances where the text speaks in an unequivocal and unqualified manner about the brothers and sisters of Jesus. For those who affirm the perpetual virginity of Mary, this creates an obvious problem. Although the 'solution' of calling these siblings stepbrothers and stepsisters is associated with Epiphanius, the 4th-century Bishop of Salamis on Cyprus, as the *Protevangelium* shows, the idea was in circulation much earlier. Ultimately the ploy of casting the siblings as children of Joseph by an earlier marriage was rejected as inadequate. In part, the growing cult of virginity in the 4th century accounts for the climate in which the 'stepbrother' explanation was rejected. Instead it was suggested that the brothers of Jesus were actually cousins and that both Joseph and Mary were perpetual virgins. The *Protevangelium* has no concern to defend the notion of the perpetual virginity of Joseph, which was a theological novelty of the 4th century. However, at every possible point it reiterates and affirms the purity and virginity of Mary prior to conceiving Jesus, at his birth, and afterwards. This is without doubt one of the most important concerns of the text.

Also in this second section readers learn the fascinating detail that Mary was responsible for weaving the curtain in the temple which would be torn from top to bottom at the moment of Jesus' death (*Prot. Jas.* 10, 12). Immediately prior to Mary's work of curtain weaving, Joseph takes himself away to build houses. This is a narrative device of convenience, since it means that her reluctant husband is removed from the scene when Mary becomes pregnant – so according to the text there is no possibility that he fathered her child.

In chapter 11, for the first time in the narrative, there is a direct parallel to events contained in the canonical infancy narratives. In line with the appearance story in Luke's Gospel, Gabriel announces Mary's forthcoming conception. In the version contained in the *Protevangelium*, Mary has the good sense to ask a few more questions – this is very helpful for the readers! Mary asks Gabriel if she will 'give birth the way women usually do' (*Prot. Jas.* 11.6). She is told 'no', but at this stage no further details are provided. On returning home, Joseph leaps to the logical conclusion that another man has been involved. Mary protests her innocence (*Prot. Jas.* 13.8), but unhelpfully, as the narrative mentioned slightly earlier, Mary had now forgotten the conversation with Gabriel (*Prot. Jas.* 12.6). No explanation is given as to how she could have failed to remember this seemingly memorable event. Yet this lack of recollection does serve to heighten the tension that develops in the story. Joseph is brought before the temple authorities and accused as being the one responsible for this heinous act. If there had been any doubt that the marriage was intended as an asexual union, the accusation that Joseph has 'violated the virgin' (*Prot. Jas.* 15.6) makes it clear that he was not expected to exercise any conjugal rites. In order to prove their innocence, both Joseph and Mary are required to undergo the 'drink test' (*Prot. Jas.* 16.3–7). This involves drinking water, journeying into the wilderness, and waiting to see if the accused returns unharmed. The outcome is positive for both, so they are acquitted of the charge. The rite seems to be a variant on the 'ritual of the water of bitterness' described in the Old Testament (Num. 5.11–31). Both husband and wife survive the test and consequently are vindicated and acquitted of the charges brought against them.

Section 3: *Prot. Jas.* 17.1–24.14

Having demonstrated the virginal conception, coupled with the declaration of Mary's pure state by the high priest, the narrative proceeds to describe the circumstances of the birth of Jesus. Here details from the two biblical accounts are interspersed within the greatly enlarged narrative of Jesus' birth. Miracles and cosmological phenomena are to be found throughout. Mary sees visions (*Prot. Jas.* 17.9), Joseph experiences the suspension of time (*Prot. Jas.* 18), the newborn infant is miraculously brought forth suckling at Mary's breast without any labour (*Prot. Jas.* 19.15–16). An examination by Salome the midwife confirms Mary's hymen is still intact – just to make the point about perpetual virginity (*Prot. Jas.* 20.2) – but because of her unbelief Salome begins to be consumed with flames (*Prot. Jas.* 20.4), and upon holding her hand out to the newborn child, Salome is healed (*Prot. Jas.* 20.8–11).

After this sequence of miracles, the narrative begins to draw more fully upon the biblical stories. In chapter 21, the visit of the magi is recounted in slightly different terms, but nearly all the major features are present – an encounter with Herod, reference to Bethlehem as the place of the Messiah's birth in accordance with scripture, the guiding star, the gifts of gold, frankincense, and myrrh, and the magi being warned in an angelic dream not to return home by the same route. Comparison of the Greek text of both the account in the Gospel of Matthew and that in the *Protevangelium* reveals extended agreements. Such similarities strongly suggest that there is a literary relationship between these two texts. Whether the author of the *Protevangelium* had a copy of Matthew (and elsewhere also Luke) in front of him, or whether he had heard those stories so often that he had internalized and virtually memorized their phrases, is impossible to tell. As the *Protevangelium* is almost unquestionably later than the canonical gospels, it is apparent that the author knew at least the two gospels by Matthew and Luke. This is not the same as claiming that the author was aware of the fourfold gospel canon, or that the two gospels which are known were bound together in the same codex. However, it does reflect a period when at the very least there was a recognition that multiple gospel accounts existed. This is again evidence that the *Protevangelium* was written no earlier than some stage in the 2nd century, after at least two of the canonical accounts.

The next three chapters provide an expansionist and fanciful account based on the tradition of Herod's 'slaughter of the innocents' (Matt. 2.16–18). These three verses from Matthew stand as the basis of a story of some 32 verses in *Protevangelium*. Herod's deployment of soldiers to execute children younger than two becomes the catalyst for the actions of two mothers. Mary simply wraps her son in strips of cloth and places Jesus in a feeding trough (*Prot. Jas.* 22.4) – a radical reinterpretation of the manger tradition. The more drastic action is taken by Elizabeth, the mother of John the Baptist. Elizabeth flees to the hill country, but when through weariness she can go no further, she cries out 'Mountain of God, please take in a mother with her child' (*Prot. Jas.* 22.7). This address to an apparently inanimate object results in the mountain splitting open and allowing this mother and child to enter in; the mountain also becomes translucent to light so Elizabeth and John are not plunged into darkness, and an angel of the Lord remains with them.

The story then moves from Elizabeth to her husband Zechariah. In accordance with the description of him in Luke's Gospel, he is found ministering in the temple. In an act of 'special rendition', Herod sends his servants to ascertain from Zechariah the whereabouts of his son. Stating his ignorance of the location of his son, Zechariah makes a martyr's speech more akin to the martyrdom accounts of the 2nd and 3rd centuries than to the purported 1st century BC context. He states, 'I am a martyr for God, take my life. The Lord though will receive my spirit because you are shedding innocent blood at the entrance to the temple of the Lord' (*Prot. Jas.* 23.7–8).

Where did such a story of the martyrdom of Zechariah, the father of John the Baptist, originate – was this pure authorial creativity? The answer is both 'yes' and 'no'. Confusion rather than fiction appears to be the basis of this tradition. In Luke 11.50–51 (cf. Matt. 23.35), there is a prophetic announcement placed on the lips of Jesus that is addressed to the inhabitants of Jerusalem: 'the blood of all the prophets, which was shed from the foundation of the world, may be required of this generation from the blood of Abel to the blood of Zacharias, who perished between the altar and the temple: truly I say unto you, it shall be required of this generation.' The identity of this 'Zechariah' remains a mystery to scholars. Most understand this as a reference to the priest Zechariah, son of Jehoiada, whom the people stone in the temple court (2 Chron. 24.20–22). In the Gospel of Matthew, the name Zechariah is qualified with 'son of Barachiah', making this a reference to the prophet Zechariah – but there is no tradition of his martyrdom. The author of the *Protevangelium* appears to have pressed this ambiguous reference into his service, by creating a martyrdom story for the father of John the Baptist and in the process further blackening the reputation of Herod and his minions. It is interesting that this demonizing of Herod does not materialize as an overt anti-Jewish sentiment in the *Protevangelium*. Instead the temple and its priests are viewed as pious agents of God. The text then concludes with a brief epilogue that describes the death of Herod and identifies the author of the text.

The value of the infancy gospels

Both the *Protevangelium of James* and the *Infancy Gospel of Thomas* are highly fictionalized accounts of stories relating to the birth, childhood, or ancestry of Jesus. Yet the value of these texts does not arise from the historicity of the events they purport to describe. Instead, these two writings, which are the earliest examples of this sub-genre of apocryphal writings, are a window onto a vibrant and diverse world of early Christianity. The way these fanciful narratives are told is both ponderous and wondrous.

At times, these stories become grindingly tedious, yet at other times they present flashes of theological insight. The bizarre, the pious, and the profound sit alongside each other in these highly creative texts. The theological purpose of the author of the *Infancy Gospel of Thomas* in creating such a maverick and fearful representation of the boy Jesus remains a mystery. By contrast, the aims of the author of the *Protevangelium of James* are generally transparent, especially when read against the backdrop of emergent Marian piety. While the historian who correctly recognizes the fictionalized portrayal of the circumstances of Mary's birth may remain unpersuaded by claims of her immaculate conception, and baulk at the pious devices to circumvent the clear meaning of references to brothers and sisters of Jesus in the canonical gospels by casting them as step-siblings, and moreover perhaps scoff at the incredulous verification of Mary's virginal state after the birth of Jesus, this does not make the texts worthless. Despite the dubious value of the historicity of the events these texts claim to record, nonetheless, they can still be appreciated as invaluable witnesses to the social and theological history of pious believers in the centuries following the life of Jesus.

Chapter 4
Gospels set during the earthly life of Jesus

Broken texts and partial lives

None of the texts considered in this chapter is complete. One is quite an extensive portion of what was obviously a larger text, although its exact range cannot be determined. Others are highly fragmentary, at best preserving a story or two that supposedly relates to the life of Jesus. Yet others are no longer existent in their own right – they are preserved through the odd fleeting reference in the writings of unsympathetic authors who do not share the perspectives of the texts they cite except for the purpose of refuting their views. So what unifies this motley collection of texts? Unlike the gospels from Nag Hammadi, they do not originate from the same cache of documents, nor like the infancy gospels do they seek to fill gaps in knowledge about the 'hidden years' of Jesus. Instead, the texts brought together here represent an arbitrary, but hopefully sensible, arrangement of material, since they recount variant or additional accounts of incidents from the earthly ministry of Jesus up until the time of his reported ascent into heaven. Hence they provide a greater overlap with the four canonical gospels than occurs with the texts previously considered. Such parallels and fresh traditions have excited some who have commented on these writings with the possibility that they may offer earlier and less theologically overlaid accounts of the life of Jesus.

Categorization choices are to some extent arbitrary and certainly contestable. The decision to include the *Gospel of Thomas* in the discussion of texts that were discovered at Nag Hammadi is, at one level, natural, but not uncontroversial. Like the vast majority of those writings, *Thomas* had a 'life' before it was collected into that corpus of writings. The existence of the various Greek fragments of *Thomas* demonstrates that some form of this text was being read in Egypt approximately 150 years prior to its incorporation into the Nag Hammadi collection. A case could undoubtedly be made for including the *Gospel of Thomas* in this chapter dealing with gospels set during the life of Jesus (although the actual setting of that sayings collection is not certain). However, because the complete form of that text is known only in the Nag Hammadi context, for pragmatic reasons, such as avoiding the complex issue of speculating about the overall shape of the Greek text, it has been decided to discuss *Thomas* in that chapter.

The *Gospel of Peter*

Archaeology and discovery of non-canonical gospels have often been closely related. Napoleon Bonaparte's interests in Egypt were not purely military. They were also aroused by intellectual and ideological motivations. His invasion of Egypt in 1798 involved a force of 35,000 military personnel embarking at Toulon, but it is often overlooked that the contingent also included 175 scholars – including archaeologists. This marked the first serious phase of the modern study of Egyptology. Initially and understandably, it was the awe-striking physical remains of that ancient culture, such as pyramids, sphinxes, and temples, which captivated scholars. The interest in the discovery of ancient texts blossomed about a century later. It was not until 1882 that efforts were formalized, with the establishment of a French Archaeological Mission in Cairo.

It was during the winter season dig of 1886/7 that a monk's grave was excavated at Akhmîm in Upper Egypt. Apart from the physical remains of the corpse, this tomb contained a small parchment codex with fragments of four texts. Although the chief excavator, Urbain Bouriant, appeared to place most emphasis on the third text (hitherto unevidenced Greek fragments of 1 Enoch), what excited the wider scholarly world was the first text – identified as the partial but fairly extensive fragment of the *Gospel of Peter*. The contents of the unusual and amateurishly compiled book were as follows:

PAGE	CONTENTS
Inside front cover	Blank
1	Decoration, religious in nature, including Coptic crosses
2–10	The *Gospel of Peter*
11–12	Blank
13–19	*Apocalypse of Peter* (but pages stitched the wrong way round and upside down, so they must be read in the order 19 to 13).
20	Blank
21–66	Two fragments from 1 Enoch
Inside back cover	*Martyrdom of St Julian*

Not all texts in this book are from the same hand. This leads to the supposition that the codex was not constructed to accommodate these four documents, but that it was put together out of fragments of previously existing documents.

Covering nine continuous pages of Greek text, the first document provided a variant version of events in the life of Jesus from his trial until the time when some of the disciples quit Jerusalem to return to their work as fishermen. At two points, the narrative breaks into a first-person account. The first time this happens, the narrator states that after the crucifixion, 'I mourned with my companions, and with disturbed senses we concealed ourselves'

(*Gos. Pet.* 7.26). Here the identity of the first-person commentator is not disclosed. The second time the use of the first-person voice occurs is in the final preserved verse of the manuscript, just before the text breaks off mid-sentence. In the aftermath of post-crucifixion events, the assumed narrator discloses his identity: 'I, Simon Peter, and my brother Andrew took our nets and went to the sea' (*Gos. Pet.* 14.60). Thus, Peter is presented as the implied narrator. Coupled with this, there exists a tradition preserved by the early Church historian Eusebius who twice mentions a gospel circulating in the name of Peter. Consequently, scholars were quick to identify the newly discovered first-person gospel-type narrative with the notice about a so-called *Gospel of Peter* contained in the writings of Eusebius. Although this is not an unreasonable assumption, caution should still be exercised, and while the identification is highly appealing, it is ultimately still a hypothesis – after all, various spurious texts survive that are written in the first person in Peter's name, which may mean that Eusebius' *Gospel of Peter* is not the same text as that discovered at Akhmîm.

Although Eusebius does not cite any actual passages from the text he knew as the *Gospel of Peter*, he does give the following important testimony about its origins, circulation, and rejection. Relating information concerning a certain Serapion, bishop of Antioch (AD 191–211), Eusebius outlines the contents of one of his writings entitled *Concerning the So-Called Gospel of Peter*. According to the source Eusebius claims to be citing, during a pastoral visit to the church of Rhossus, without examining its contents Serapion initially permitted the reading of the *Gospel of Peter*. Upon returning to Antioch, after being informed of the contents of this document, he reversed his decision.

> But since I have now learnt, from what has been told me, that their
> mind was lurking in some hole of heresy, I shall give diligence to
> come again to you; wherefore, brethren, expect me quickly. But we,
> brethren, gathering to what kind of heresy Marcianus belonged
> (who used to contradict himself, not knowing what he was saying, as

you will learn from what has been written to you), were enabled by others who studied this very Gospel, that is, by the successors of those who began it, whom we call Docetae (for most of the ideas belong to their teaching) – using the materials supplied by them, were enabled to go through it and discover that the most part indeed was in accordance with the true teaching of the Saviour, but that some things were added, which also we place below for your benefit.

(see *H.E.* 6.12.3–6)

Unfortunately Eusebius does not replicate Serapion's list of added elements.

The term 'docetic' derives from a Greek word meaning appearance or semblance. It came to be used as a technical term to describe an understanding of the person of Christ that was deemed to be inadequate by emergent 'orthodox' Christians. As previously mentioned, docetism emphasized that the divine Logos inhabited the body of Jesus of Nazareth in order to veil its presence, but without become truly united with the human form. Prior to the crucifixion, the divine being left the human shell. This was necessary since the Logos was beyond suffering. According to Eusebius' convoluted sentences, it appears that the *Gospel of Peter* was not itself considered to be docetic (although some of the 'added things' may have been), but rather that it was used by those Serapion labelled as 'docetae' to support their own teachings.

Notwithstanding this distinction, part of the early scholarly analysis of this text involved identifying features which were seen as aligning with docetism. For those who wished to unearth docetic elements in the text discovered at Akhmîm, they felt no need to look beyond the only words spoken by Jesus in the entire nine pages of text. Instead of the familiar cry of dereliction found in the gospels of Matthew and Mark, 'my God, my God why have you forsaken me?' (Matt. 27.46/Mark 15.34), the *Gospel of Peter* places the following words on the lips of Jesus: 'My power, the power, you have forsaken me' (*Gos. Pet.* 5.19). For many scholars, this acknowledgement of the power leaving Jesus read like the divine Logos leaving the human shell to suffer. However, this reading simply will not do. First, the 'power' leaves after all the suffering has taken place – beatings, whippings, and crucifixion. Second, it occurs at the point of death, when it is natural to speak of one's life-force or power leaving one. Last, the traditional words – 'my God, my God why have you forsaken me?' – are highly problematic. They create a picture of a despairing Jesus, who genuinely feels abandoned by God. The theological disquiet this could cause is already demonstrated by Luke's not too subtle rewriting of this cry as the irenic 'Father into your hands I commit my spirit' (Luke 23.46). Similarly, the *Gospel of Peter*, by rewording the cry, also avoids a theological problem, and instead has Jesus almost prophetically identify the moment of his death. This may be an expedient authorial strategy, but it does not really look like an attempt to smuggle docetic perspectives into the Jesus story.

So if the purpose is not to give a docetic version of the Passion, what is the purpose of the text? In fact, there are a number of different agendas at work here as the text gently slants the Passion story in various ways. The miracle tradition is radically heightened. Like many Christian texts written in this pre-scientific period, the accounts of miracles are seen as a source of encouragement to believers and a means of commending the faith to outsiders. While the more philosophically minded contemporary critics of early Christianity could characterize such stories as mere superstitions or old wives' tales, the vast majority of the population was credulous and was swayed by accounts of the miraculous.

The miracles contained in the *Gospel of Peter* both develop stories known from the canonical accounts to make them even more striking and add miraculous signs unattested in the four canonical gospels. The most famous newly innovated series of miracles in the *Gospel of Peter* occurs when Jesus is led forth from the tomb. First, two 'men' descend from heaven, and automatically the stone at the entrance to the tomb rolls away as the men approach (*Gos. Pet.*

9.36–37). When they leave the tomb, they are supporting a third man between them. The bodily dimensions of all three have been transformed. The two who descended have heads that 'reach to the heavens, but that of the one led by them reached beyond the heavens' (*Gos. Pet.* 10.40). However, the most outlandish and captivating miracle comes in response to a divine question. When the voice from heaven enquires, 'Have you preached to those who are asleep?', contrary to what might be expected it is not Jesus who responds. Instead, the cross which followed the three men out of the tomb answers 'yes!' This can be described as an embellishment to the canonical tradition. For those interested in the development of Christian traditions, this is one of the earliest examples of 'cross-piety' – a type of devotion that focuses on contemplation of the cross of Jesus. Walking and talking visions of the cross are not frequent, but they do occur in some other later texts. The tradition of the so-called 'harrowing of hell', prominent in late antique and early medieval texts, often results in the cross of Christ being left planted in hell as an emblematic sign of victory over death as Christ himself leads forth all the Old Testament figures from the bonds of Hades into heaven. While miracles such as talking and walking crosses are bizarre to the sensibilities of many people living in a modern scientific culture, they are commonplace and evolve in vivid ways in early Christian tradition.

Blame-shifting is also a key feature of the *Gospel of Peter*. In the canonical gospels, both the Romans (represented in the figure of Pilate) and the Jewish leaders shoulder the blame for the crucifixion of Jesus. By contrast, in the *Gospel of Peter* Pilate becomes an advocate for Jesus, even if his portrayal as subservient to Herod Antipas ensures that he is not able to prevent the crucifixion. The other side of this re-portrayal results in Herod Antipas, Jewish leaders, and the Jewish mob in Jerusalem being represented as playing a much greater role in the death of Jesus. Such a phenomenon reflects wider Christian practice of heightening the involvement of the Jewish people in perpetrating the death of Jesus, to exonerate the Romans, thereby removing the stigma that Jesus had been executed under the judicial authority of the imperial system, and consequently to create a greater divide between Judaism and Christianity than was actually the reality of the origins of the 1st-century Jesus movement.

P.Cair. 10759 f.1r

10. The opening page of the codex containing the *Gospel of Peter*. The decorative artwork consists of three Coptic crosses and the religiously symbolic letters alpha and omega

11. **The opening two pages of the text of the *Gospel of Peter*. At the top of the first page there is an**

12. The final page of the manuscript of the *Gospel of Peter*. The text finishes mid-sentence. The scribe, however, had space at the foot of the page to add ornamental decorations – three Coptic crosses and a patterned embellishment. Also the following page is left blank. This suggests that the scribe broke off mid-sentence because he was copying a text which itself was incomplete, since the decision to cease writing was not due to space constraints

A further aim of the text is apologetic. In Matthew's Gospel, it is reported that 'the Jews' had circulated the story that the disciples had stolen the body from the tomb in order to fabricate the resurrection. According to Matthew, the true origin of the rumour is that the Jewish authorities bribed the guard at the tomb to circulate this story in order to cover up the resurrection. Other early Christian writers in the 2nd and 3rd centuries responded to this same accusation. A major portion of the *Gospel of Peter* retells a highly expanded version of this story in a way that undercuts the charge of the disciples stealing the body themselves. This means the text has a strongly apologetic flavour, defending the Christian faith against perceived points of weakness or susceptibility.

Contents

The text of the *Gospel of Peter* begins, as it ends, in the middle of a broken sentence. Modern scholars have divided it into 14 chapters (with a further subdivision into 60 verses). This helpfully enables the discussion of individual scenes. The first partially preserved scene would appear to follow on from a detail found only in Matthew's Gospel – the moment when Pilate famously washes his hands and declares 'I am innocent of this man's blood' (Matt. 27.24). The first surviving line of the text of the *Gospel of Peter* states 'but of the Jews no one washed the hands, nor Herod, nor one of his judges. And when they were not willing to wash, Pilate rose up' (*Gos. Pet.* 1.1). This expansion of the canonical tradition presents the behaviour of the Jewish authority figures as being in contrast with that of Pilate, who rises up in protest against the miscarriage of justice that he is viewing. Next Joseph enters the scene. Although he is not named explicitly as the Joseph of Arimithea known from the accounts of Matthew, Luke, and John, there can be little doubt that the same figure is intended, since he undertakes the same task of requesting the body of Jesus from Pilate. However, unlike the sequence of the canonical narratives, this request is made prior to the crucifixion rather than afterwards.

Presumably this is primarily a stylistic alteration which makes space for the additional details the author of the *Gospel of Peter* introduces to the post-crucifixion storyline. In chapter 3, a description of the pre-crucifixion mockery takes place. Not only is this more brutal than that of the canonical gospels, but it is carried out by the Jewish mob acting at the behest of Herod Antipas rather than by Roman soldiers acting in accordance with Pilate's orders. Thus a controlled Roman execution is transformed into a brutal act of mob violence. This is carried out under the direction of Herod Antipas. The effect is to shift the blame away from the Romans and to implicate 'Jews' more fully in the crucifixion of Jesus.

Chapter 4 commences the crucifixion scene proper. Interestingly, the title on the cross is not 'This is the King of the Jews' (Luke 23.58), but is subtly altered to 'This is the King of Israel' (*Gos. Pet.* 4.11). Whereas the term 'Jew' had become pejorative, early Christians wished to claim the heritage of historic Israel as their own. The same tendency was found in the *Infancy Gospel of Thomas*, where the supposed author describes himself as 'Thomas the Israelite' (*Inf. Gos. Thom.* 1.1). This section of the *Gospel of Peter* also shows its dependence on Luke's account by retelling the story of the penitent thief, which among the canonical gospels only occurs in Luke. However, the *Gospel of Peter* piously deletes the reference to one of the two criminals reviling Jesus. Thus a more reverential attitude towards protecting the status of Jesus is to be detected. In the ensuing description of the crucifixion, accompanying miracles become more fabulous and the apocalyptic portents are more vivid. The darkness that descends is coupled with a description of people stumbling around with lamps. The earthquake which occurs at the point of Jesus' death, recorded in Matt. 27.51, takes place in the *Gospel of Peter* precisely at the moment when the sacred body of Jesus is taken down and laid on the ground. The earth itself convulses upon coming into contact with this corpse. No thoroughgoing docetic theology would view the dead shell of the divine Logos in such reverential terms.

The remainder of the account relates post-crucifixion events. Bemused and trembling onlookers, cowering disciples, and devious Jewish officials pepper the narrative. The story of the guard at the tomb is greatly developed in comparison to the version in Matthew's account. Contrasting with that shorter version, in the *Gospel of Peter* the Jewish authorities anticipate the possibility of the disciples stealing the body prior to the resurrection. Proactive action is taken. Pilate is approached for a detachment of guards to secure the site. A huge stone is rolled in place to block the entrance, seven seals are affixed, and a tent is pitched so that round-the-clock surveillance can take place. The extraordinary anticipatory security is obviously a mythical feature of this story, which simultaneously rebuts claims that the disciples could have snatched the body while also showing that only divine intervention would be able to breach such defences. The emphasis placed on these features reveals that the text had the apologetic purpose to nullify the suggestion that disciples came to an unguarded tomb, took the body, and consequently created a resurrection myth. Thus, the *Gospel of Peter* tells the story in such a way as to undercut such an argument.

In a story full of miraculous interference and written for those who knew the outline of the canonical accounts, the events of the resurrection are not unanticipated. However, they have certainly become more fantastic. Trembling soldiers, descending angels, a self-animated stone, enlarged bodies, and a walking and talking cross – liberties are definitely taken with the more primitive form of the story. Yet this probably illustrates the attitudes of those who used the canonical texts to teach such traditions. The text was a resource for theological reflection, not a fixed and invariable entity – at least for the author of the *Gospel of Peter*, and he certainly was not alone in this attitude. Other texts from this period exhibit a similar tendency.

The last sections of the text conclude with a declaration from Pilate that he is 'clean from the blood of the Son of God' (*Gos. Pet.* 11.46).

This proclamation of innocence not only absolves Pilate, but has the purpose of shifting the blood-guilt for the death of Jesus squarely onto the Jewish people. However, out of fear of the crowds, the leaders reason that 'it is better for us to make ourselves guilty of the greatest sin before God than to fall into the hands of the people of the Jews and be stoned' (*Gos. Pet.* 11.48). While such tendencies are understandable historically as Christians sought to define their own identity in what was at times bitter opposition to Jewish rivals, the consequences of such a 'blame-game' theology have resulted in some of the most reprehensible acts of anti-Jewish persecution by Christians. Obviously the *Gospel of Peter* is not solely or even primarily responsible for this. It does, however, represent an early expression of the anti-Jewish attitude which was to flower into the bitter fruit of medieval pogroms against Jews, and even might have shaped the thinking that could have led to supposed Christians turning a blind-eye or even worse during the events of the 20th-century Holocaust.

The narrative continues before it breaks off with a number of post-resurrection events. The story from Mark's Gospel of the visit of the women to the tomb is followed in fairly close detail – although there are embellishments. The narrative ends with the beginnings of a story in which Simon Peter and Andrew are fishing beside the sea, perplexed and uncertain what to do after Jesus' death. Here it appears that a story similar to that contained in the final chapter of John's Gospel will be recounted. Yet, unless somebody unearths another manuscript of this fascinating text, this may remain a supposition – admittedly a highly plausible one, but a supposition nonetheless.

The ongoing value of the *Gospel of Peter*

Despite the outlandish miracles it contains, in many ways the *Gospel of Peter* is one of the more approachable non-canonical gospels to read. It covers a familiar story, admittedly in an embellished and expanded manner, but it does not rely on coded language or speculative cosmologies like some of the gospel texts found at Nag Hammadi. It has multiple purposes. Gap-filling is a primary aim: that is, telling the Jesus story in a way that supplies missing details or removes difficulties in the storyline of the canonical writings in order to produce a more internally consistent account.

Some recent scholars working on this text have claimed that it preserves a form of the Passion narrative which is in fact earlier than the form contained in the canonical gospels. The more sophisticated version of this theory was advanced by J. D. Crossan, who suggested that the *Gospel of Peter* as it survives has embedded within it an early Passion narrative source, which Crossan dubs 'the Cross Gospel'. After removing material that is regarded as dependent on the canonical accounts, such as the visit of the women to the tomb which occurs towards the end of the *Gospel of Peter* (12.50–13.57) and is seen as dependent on Mark (16.1–8), the resultant material is viewed as more primitive than the synoptic gospels and as being a source used by them. Two factors tell against this theory. First, even within the material that is left in the hypothetical 'Cross Gospel', there appear to be elements that are still dependent on canonical sources, such as the story of the thief on the cross (*Gos. Pet.* 4.10–14; cf. Luke 23.39–43). Second, the actual preserved text of the *Gospel of Peter* does not appear to have the kind of disjunctions that usually point to such literary seams. In other words, there is little within the text to support the type of source theory suggested by Crossan.

A less nuanced version of this theory is presented by Paul Mirecki. He claims that the entire *Gospel of Peter* pre-dates the material in the canonical accounts: 'The *Gospel of Peter* (= *Gos. Pet.*) was a narrative gospel of the synoptic type which circulated in the mid-1st century under the authority of the name Peter. An earlier form of the gospel probably served as one of the major sources for the canonical gospels.' This claim falls foul of the obvious places where the *Gospel of Peter* is dependent on canonical sources which were written after the mid-1st century. Not only is it possible to detect clear parallels between the canonical stories and the version contained in the text discovered at Akhmîm, but the parallels in the *Gospel of Peter* appear derivative of the canonical gospels, and moreover its theological concerns reflect the known developments of Christian thinking traceable to the 2nd and 3rd centuries.

Therefore, this text is no repository of unadulterated historical information concerning the crucifixion of Jesus. Instead, it is heavily overlaid with anti-Jewish sentiment, apologetic concerns, and a desire to weave together details from the canonical gospels. Its does attest to the way in which later generations of early Christians handled the Jesus tradition as transmitted in the canonical gospels, and it shows how those traditions could be tailored to address the theological concerns of the period in which the text was formed. Like a thoughtful contemporary preacher, the author of the *Gospel of Peter* makes the story of Jesus speak to the concerns and needs of the current situation of his early Christian audience.

Papyrus Oxyrhynchus 840

The unbelievably rich troves of papyrus manuscripts discovered at Oxyrhynchus and the highly significant fragments of the *Gospel of Thomas* have already been mentioned, but a number of other important fragmentary texts were also discovered. For illustrative purposes only, one example will be discussed here. Papyrus Oxyrhynchus 840 (P.Oxy. 840) records an otherwise unattested story of Jesus that supposedly stems from the period of Jesus' ministry on an occasion when he visited the Jerusalem temple. Because of its brevity, the full text of this fragment can be provided:

Papyrus Oxyrhynchus 840

'... earlier, before doing wrong, he slyly reasons everything out. Be careful that you do not end up suffering the same fate as them. For the evil-doers of humanity receive retribution not only among the living, but they will also undergo punishment and much torture later.'

Taking them along, he went into the place of purification itself and wandered around in the temple. Then a certain high priest of the Pharisees named Levi came toward them and said to the saviour, 'Who permitted you to wander in this place of purification and to see these holy vessels, even though you have not bathed, and the feet of your disciples have not been washed? And now that you have defiled it, you walk around in this pure area of the temple where only a person who has bathed and changed his clothes can walk, and even such a person does not dare to look upon these holy vessels.'

Standing nearby with his disciples, the saviour replied, 'Since you are here in the temple too, are you clean?'

The Pharisee said to him, 'I am clean for I bathed in the pool of David. I went down into the pool by one set of stairs and came back out by another. Then I put on white clothes and they were clean. And then I came and looked at these holy vessels.'

Replying to him, the saviour said, 'Woe to blind people who do not see! You have washed in the gushing waters that dogs and pigs are thrown into day and night. And when you washed yourself, you scrubbed the outer layer of skin, the layer of skin that prostitutes and flute-girls anoint and wash and scrub when they put on make up to become the desire of the men. But inside they are filled with scorpions and all unrighteousness. But my disciples and I, whom you say have not washed, we have washed in waters of eternal life that come from the God of heaven. But woe to those . . .'

This fragmentary text is written front to back on a single vellum leaf, of unusually small size. The dimensions are approximately 7.4 by 8.8 centimetres. There has been ongoing debate about whether this is a leaf from a longer miniature codex, or whether the leaf was an amulet worn by its owner to ward off evil. It contains two partial preserved stories. The end of the first story is brief and no context can be determined. It comprises an apocalyptic judgment saying directed against 'evil-doers of humanity'. This saying, presumably spoken by Jesus, exhorts his hearers to guard themselves against suffering the same fate as the evil-doers. Little more can be said about this first story.

The second is much more fully preserved and comprises context, narrative, and dialogue. Set within the precincts of the Jerusalem temple, Jesus and his disciples are engaged in a debate with the high priest about purity requirements. The charge levelled against Jesus and his companions is that they have transgressed the holiness of 'the place of purification' and viewed the 'holy vessels' without undergoing the prerequisite ablutions. Jesus' reply affirms the facts of the high priest's charge, but denies the implications drawn from it. Reversing the accusation, Jesus asks the high priest if he is clean. The response given by the high priest is a standard recitation of the formal steps taken to ensure purity. Jesus attacks this perspective on two levels. First, he states the very water in which the high priest washed was itself polluted since it had been contaminated by the uncleanness of dogs and pigs. Whether this is meant to be understood literally, or whether 'dogs and pigs' is a metaphor for unclean people, is uncertain. Second, the lustrations undertaken by the high priest are criticized for dealing only with superficial exterior purification. By contrast, Jesus calls for an internal purification, whereby one is cleansed with the metaphorical waters of eternal life. Such controversy stories are evidenced within the canonical gospels, although in this case it must be admitted that the likelihood of a chance encounter between Jesus and a high priest seems remote. Moreover, no high priest by the name of Levi is known from other sources for the entire time from the Persian period down to the destruction of the temple in AD 70.

Observations such as the last one raise a number of potential difficulties encountered in this text. The location of 'the place of purification' and the location of the 'holy vessels' have been hotly debated. It has been questioned whether the latter, which may denote the candelabrum, the altar of incense, and table of showbread, could ever be viewed by people who were not members of the priestly caste. It has been suggested recently that historically this is not an insurmountable problem since, according to the Jewish historian Josephus, during certain special times of the year the restrictions on viewing the vessels were temporarily suspended, and the curtain of the tabernacle was rolled back so that the people could view the interior. An even greater problem has been that there is no evidence of a requirement for visitors to the temple to completely immerse in a bath prior to entry. Such difficulties have led to other approaches to this text.

Alternatively, it has been suggested that this story does not reflect actual historical practices in the Jerusalem temple, but rather it fits better into ancient Christian disputes about the validity of water baptism. If this is correct, then the text stems from an ecclesial controversy of the 2nd or 3rd centuries and does not provide a window onto actual events in the life of Jesus during the 1st century. A third mediating option is to take the text as historizing, but not historical. By this it is meant that while the text may claim to report actual events from the life of Jesus, it is creatively written at some significantly later time and consequently might contain historical anachronisms. From this perspective, the text may, or may not, be addressing baptismal controversies.

Names or titles applied to Jesus can be revealing about the possible authorship and readers of such texts. Throughout this brief fragment, Jesus is described as 'the saviour' and no other title or name is used for him. Although used widely in early Christianity, the title 'saviour' is also prominent in texts like the *Gospel of Philip*. By noting such links, it has been suggested that the text has been written from a 'Gnostic' perspective to counter either Jewish–Christian baptist movements or mainstream Christian promotion of baptism as the only necessary entrance rite. While such theories do draw upon the link that existed in some texts that use the title 'saviour' and also see baptism as only the basic entrance ritual, they do not explain the fact that P.Oxy. 840 is not laden with the type of cosmological reflections that are so often characteristic of Gnostic texts.

P.Oxy. 840 is a fascinating but often overlooked text. The main incident it relates does have the same kind of 'feel' as many of the canonical controversy stories. However, there does seem to be an inordinate number of historically anachronistic details. This leads to the suspicion that the author was trying to imitate the style and genre of the controversies story, and while largely successful, left traces of historically implausible details that reveal that this narrative was created in a period somewhat later than the life of Jesus, and is not drawn from an historical source but rather reflects the author's imaginative invention. What could the purpose of the story be? Perhaps it does relate to an internal Christian baptismal controversy. This is not totally obvious, especially as the primary interlocutor is a Pharisaic priest and not a fellow disciple. It is more likely that the text reflects the larger Christian agenda of polemicizing against Judaism. The key accusation is that strict observance of the Jewish law results only in superficial purity and not in the more important internal cleansing of one's being. While such a critique of formulaic Torah observance can be found within Judaism itself – especially in the writings of the prophets – this charge seems to have been appropriated by Christians as a ready-made way of critiquing the Jewish faith.

An 'unknown gospel': Papyrus Egerton 2

'Not since the discovery of the Sayings of Jesus at Oxyrhynchus has a Christian papyrus come to light which raises so many and such interesting problems as the present fragments.' Thus opens the 1935 discussion of Papyrus Egerton 2 in the critical edition of these fragments published a year after they had been purchased from an antiquities dealer. That publication presented an edition of four fragments from three or four leaves of a codex – this can be determined because they are written on both sides of the papyrus leaves. Deciphering the fragments and determining their relative ordering is a problem not dissimilar to a jigsaw puzzle. The fourth fragment consists of a single letter – probably a sigma, but uncertain – and since this cannot be located in relation to the other fragments, it is of no help in determining the text. The third fragment is somewhat larger, 6.0 by 2.3 centimetres, but contains only a few words and hence is also too small to assist the overall reconstruction of the text. The remaining two fragments of single-column text are somewhat larger: Fragment 1: 11.5 by 9.2 centimetres, Fragment 2: 11.8 by 9.7 centimetres. These two fragments offer enough text to enable at least a partially coherent reconstruction. The story of the fragments of this text did not end with the 1935 critical edition.

More than 50 years later, another fragment of the same manuscript was discovered in a collection of papyri housed in Cologne. This fragment, measuring 5.5 by 3.0 centimetres, was seen as belonging to the same leaf as Fragment 1. On both the front and back of this new fragment of the same leaf were preserved five partial lines of text. This new fragment assisted completing two lines that were already partially extant in Fragment 1, as well as providing parts of three further lines. This combination of fragments now means that strictly speaking the text should be referred to as Papyrus Egerton 2 + Papyrus Cologne 255. Examination of the Cologne fragment has also resulted in an adjustment to the dating. In their 1935 edition, Bell and Skeat stated that it was 'extremely improbable' that Papyrus Egerton 2 'can be dated later than the middle of the second century'. Taking into account the physical features of the Cologne fragment, the dating of the manuscript has been revised, it now being generally accepted that the codex is to be dated around AD 200. This is based upon the presence of a diacritical sign (an apostrophe) of a type frequently attested in the 3rd century but not the 2nd.

A fundamental problem with these two fragments (Fragment 1 + P.Cologne 255, and Fragment 2) is their relative ordering – which one preceded the other, and the even more basic question of which side of each fragment should be read first. The conventional way of arranging these texts is Fragment 1 *verso*, Fragment 1 *recto*, Fragment 2 *verso*, Fragment 2 *recto*, which are here presented and discussed in that order.

[…] And Jesus said to the lawyers: 'Punish every wrongdoer and transgressor, and not me. […] he does, how does he do it?'

And turning to the rulers of the people he said this word: 'Search the scriptures, in which you think you have life. These are they, which testify about me. Do not suppose that I have come to accuse you to my father. There is one who accuses you: Moses, in whom you have hoped.'

And they said: 'We know that God spoke to Moses, but as for you, we do not know, where you are from.'

Jesus answered and said to them: 'Now is accused your disbelief in those who have been commended by him. For had you believed Moses, you would have believed me. For about me he wrote to your fathers […]'

This brief incident portrays Jesus in polemical dialogue with two named groups of people – 'the lawyers' and 'the rulers of the people'. Against the first group, Jesus appears to be responding to an accusation that he is a transgressor by affirming the right of the lawyers to punish wrong-doers, but refuting their charge that Jesus himself falls into that category. The second part of this fragment involves the confrontation with the rulers concerning whether or not the scriptures testify to Jesus, and whether Jesus or the rulers can claim the authority of Moses as an ally for their respective stances. The wording in this narrative is extremely close to passages from John's Gospel at a number of points. In John 5.39, Jesus informs his opponents, 'you search the scriptures, because you think that in them you have eternal life, and it is these that bear witness to me'. A few verses later in John's account, Jesus tells his adversaries 'do not think that I shall accuse you before the Father, the one who accuses you is Moses, in whom you have set your hope' (John 5.45). There are also partial parallels with material from John 9.29. Yet, despite these striking agreements, here Papyrus Egerton 2 preserves a number of independent features in the story. It is impossible to tell whether the author recycled the story from the Gospel of John to mould his own version, or if he knew the sayings in a form that was earlier than John's narrative, and consequently he preserves a more primitive version of the tradition. Nonetheless, in both versions the same key idea is communicated – the scriptures need to be read eschatologically in light of Jesus' coming. He is the interpretative key to the meaning within scripture, and hence Moses can be seen as a witness who verifies the claims Jesus makes about himself.

Fragment 1 *recto*

[…] and taking up stones together to stone him. And the rulers laid their hands upon him to seize him and hand him over to the crowd. And they could not take him because the hour of his arrest had not yet come. But the Lord himself, escaping from their hands, withdrew from them.

And behold, a leper coming to him, says: 'Teacher Jesus, while travelling with lepers and eating together with them in the inn, I myself also became a leper. If therefore you will, I am clean.' And the Lord said to him: 'I will, be clean.'

And immediately the leprosy left him. And Jesus said to him: 'Go show yourself to the priests and offer concerning the cleansing as Moses commanded and sin no more […]'

This section of the text again preserves the remains of two stories. The first is the end of a scene where presumably the crowd are seeking to stone Jesus and the rulers are willing to be complicit in this action, by trying to seize Jesus and to hand him over to the mob. The reason for this desire to murder Jesus is not preserved in the surviving section of the narrative, but if the *verso* of this fragment provides any clue it could be due to the elevated claims Jesus is making about his status and his identity with the Father. This is also supported by the wider context of the parallel passage in John 7 and 8. In John 7.28–30, Jesus claims that he is the Father's appointed envoy and that his origin is with the Father. In response, the rulers 'were seeking to seize him, and no man laid his hand upon him because his hour had not yet come'. Similarly, in John 8.58–59, 'the Jews' pick up stones to stone Jesus. In that context the intended murderous plan stems from Jesus' declaration that 'before Abraham was, I am' (John 8.58). The 'I am' claim is not just poor grammar, nor is it only a claim to existence prior to Abraham, but more provocatively it seems to be an attempt by Jesus to appropriate the divine name Yahweh, which may mean something like 'I am'. Although Papyrus Egerton 2 does not preserve either of these contexts, the similar responses are suggestive that Jesus' Christological sayings may form the preceding context of this fragment.

The second story records the healing of a leper. It is reminiscent of the account in Mark 1.40–45; see also the parallels in Matt. 8.2–4 and Luke 5.12–14. In the versions of this story in Matthew and Luke, the leper addresses Jesus as 'Lord', here the title used is 'teacher'. This may show that the version of the story preserved in Papyrus Egerton 2 originated in a section of the early Jesus movement where the title 'Lord' was problematic. The saying in Matt. 7.21 attests this kind of disquiet over addressing Jesus as 'Lord': 'not every one who says to me "Lord, Lord" will enter into the kingdom of heaven, but he who does the will of my Father who is in heaven'. While there are striking similarities between this version of the story and those contained in the canonical accounts, again the differences reveal a version of the story that sets its own agenda and priorities. Interestingly, the story appears to introduce the novelistic detail that the leper contracted the disease while travelling with lepers and eating with them at an inn. The final instructions given by Jesus both preserve the canonical version, but also supplement it. In line with law-observance, the cleansing is to be recognized by a priest – hence the command to show oneself to the priest and make the required offering. However, the command to 'sin no more' is not part of the original story. Rather, it recollects a saying that occurs twice: in John's Gospel (John 5.14); and also in the floating tradition of the women caught in adultery that attached itself to John's Gospel (see John 8.11). Again elements from John's Gospel are discernible.

The *verso* of Fragment 2 is in poor shape. The manuscript is in bad repair and there are no obvious canonical parallels to assist the reconstruction of this text. For these reasons, few comments have been offered by those studying this section of the text.

Fragment 2 *recto*

Coming to him, they tested him in an exacting way, saying: 'Teacher Jesus, we know that you have come from God, for what you do testifies beyond all the prophets. Therefore tell us, is it lawful to pay to kings the things which benefit their rule? Shall we pay them or not?'

But Jesus, perceiving their purpose and becoming indignant said to them: 'Why do you call me teacher with your mouth, not doing what I say? Well did Isaiah prophesy concerning you, saying: "This people honour me with their lips, but their heart is far from me. And in vain they worship me, teaching as their doctrines the precepts of men ..." '

Interestingly, this fragment also preserves a scene of confrontation between Jesus and unnamed opponents. The repeated occurrence of controversy stories and scenes of conflict between Jesus and opponents over claims of status and issues of law-observance may suggest something about the profile of this text. Although the amount of evidence is limited, and consequently suggestions about purpose and origins must be made with great caution and by acknowledging their tentative status, it may be the case that this text originated in Jewish–Christian circles with the aim of portraying Jesus as Torah-observant. Moreover, the text upholds Jesus' claims about his own status on the basis of Mosaic witness and the testimony of scripture.

Papyrus Egerton 2 is significant for two further reasons. First, it is a very early example of the Christian preference for writing texts in codex form rather than on scrolls. Second, it is one of the earliest examples of the practice of using *nomina sacra*. This is a form of abbreviating various words such as 'Lord', 'Jesus', 'Christ', and 'God' in Christian texts. This is usually done by contraction: that is, writing simply the first and last letters of these words with a horizontal (or supralinear) stroke above the letters. A debate continues among scholars as to whether the practice reflected Jewish scribal habits in treating the divine name as sacred, as in making sure that one avoided pronouncing the name 'Yahweh', or if it was simply a technique for abbreviating words with a high rate of repetition. It is noteworthy that besides the usual words abbreviated this way, Papyrus Egerton 2 also uses the technique to abbreviate 'Father', 'Moses', 'Isaiah', and 'Prophets'. While this text does not resolve the larger debate, it does seem to reflect an early phase of the practice prior to the convention becoming standardized, and hence it shows greater freedom in its abbreviation forms.

Papyrus Egerton 2 is an early Christian manuscript most likely written around AD 200. It may transmit a text that was written several decades earlier, but the difficulties in arriving at a plausible date of composition must be acknowledged. While many have noted the number of independent elements in its fragmentary text, the number of sayings with parallels contained in the Gospel of John suggests that the author knew and recycled material from that source. Again, close analysis suggests that this non-canonical gospel does not offer Jesus traditions that are earlier than the canonical gospels. Instead, it attests to a common and oft-repeated tendency among the non-canonical gospels – that of taking up material from the canonical gospels and freely and creatively reworking those stories and sayings.

The Jewish–Christian gospels

No manuscript is preserved from this group of gospel texts. Their titles are known only through mention in the work of various other early Christian writers. Occasionally these writers also quote a snippet of a tradition from these documents. Through these scant remains one is left with at best a partial impression of the wording of these texts and some of the theological concerns they may have embodied.

The very term 'Jewish-Christian' requires some explanation. The origin of the early Jesus movement was embedded in the matrix of Judaism. Jesus commenced his public ministry in Galilee, was crucified in Jerusalem, and it was in that same city that many of his relatives and early disciples continued the movement in his name. These people were Jews, they observed the Jewish law, they maintained the kosher dietary codes, refrained from work on the Sabbath, and were cautious about contact with Gentiles. Yet they differed from many of their fellow Jews in their belief that Jesus of Nazareth, the one put to death with the shameful execution of crucifixion, was paradoxically God's chosen Messiah.

This messianic faction within Judaism was radically transformed by a number of early missionaries who preached this message outside the frontiers of Judea, initially to diaspora Jews in local synagogues. Their preaching not only attracted Jewish converts, but proved surprisingly popular among Gentiles. A dilemma faced the early movement, namely whether Gentile converts were required to observe the Jewish law, or whether there could be a 'law-free' version of Christianity for Gentiles. In essence, 'law-free' Christianity for most Gentile believers did not mean cutting all links with Jewish traditions and scriptures. Rather, what was at stake was the necessity of maintaining some of the more obvious boundary-marking practices of Judaism. The three major issues were circumcision, Sabbath observance, and maintenance of dietary laws. Different answers were formulated in various sectors of the movement in regard to the necessity for Gentile converts to uphold these traditional marks of Judaism. The rulings of the Jerusalem Church under the leadership of James, Jesus' brother, were particularly influential. This group was more conservative in its understanding of the need to maintain some form of adherence to the law on the part of Gentiles than the more liberal-minded Paul, who portrayed himself as apostle to the Gentiles. However, the martyrdom of James coupled with the destruction of Jerusalem in AD 70 meant this powerful group in the early Jesus movement was widely scattered in the aftermath of the Jewish War with Rome, had lost its cohesion, and was being swamped by the increasing numbers of Gentile converts. The most influential authority group in the earliest phase of the Jesus movement had lost most of its power-base and had become pushed to the margins – yet it had not totally vanished, nor was it totally silenced.

The literary remains of this movement are scant and, as has been described, what remains are merely floating sayings or brief narratives embedded in the works of other authors. Since many of those authors refer to the 'Jewish–Christian' gospels in a variety of ways, there is debate between scholars as to how many such texts existed. From the surviving fragments, scholars have argued for either two or three gospel texts. These are usually referred to under the following titles: the *Gospel according to the Hebrews*, the *Gospel of the Nazoraeans*, and the *Gospel of the Ebionites*. The last two titles are modern constructs used to designate material that ancient sources attribute to the Nazoraean or Ebionite groups respectively, but without giving the literary title from which the material was taken. By contrast, the ancient sources directly name a *Gospel according to the Hebrews*. The majority position is that there were three discrete documents; however, others argue that the material that some have classified as belonging to *Nazoraeans* was actually part of *Hebrews*, and hence see only two Jewish-Christian gospels.

The earliest direct evidence for the existence of a Jewish–Christian gospel comes from three Christian writers who lived in the second largest city in the Roman Empire, Alexandria in Egypt: Clement of Alexandria, Origen, and Didymus the Blind. These figures spanned different periods from the late 2nd century to the beginning of the 4th century. Their combined references to the *Gospel according to the Hebrews* suggest that this Jewish–Christian gospel enjoyed a certain longevity in Alexandria, perhaps due to the presence of a large and diverse Jewish population. By contrast, most of the material identified as belonging to the *Gospel of the Nazoraeans* comes from a single source – Jerome's *Commentary on Matthew*. Jerome presents a number of traditions in his *Commentary* which he claims to have translated from a Hebrew or Aramaic source into Greek.

> The Gospel called according to the Hebrews which was recently translated by me into Greek and Latin, which Origin frequently uses, records the resurrection of the Saviour.
>
> And when the Lord had given the linen cloth to the servant of the priest, he went to James and appeared to him. For James had sworn that he would not eat bread from the hour in which he had drunk the cup of the Lord until he should see him risen from among them that sleep. And shortly thereafter the Lord said: Bring a table and bread! And immediately it is added: he took the bread, blessed it and brake it and gave it to James the Just and said to him: My brother, eat your bread, for the Son of Man is risen from among them that sleep.
>
> (Jerome, *Vir. Inl.* 2)

Likewise, the *Gospel of the Ebionites* has a single witness. Epiphanius, in his work entitled the *Panarion* ('medicine-chest'), seeks to provide readers with 'remedies' against the various 'heresies' circulating in Christianity. In chapter 30 of this work, he cites from a gospel used by the Ebionite. There is strong evidence to suggest that this work was composed in Greek, due to the presence of a pun that works only in that language. Although the text is most closely aligned with traditions from Matthew, it combines elements from Luke's Gospel at a number of points and this text may be best considered as a type of gospel harmony. Epiphanius preserves seven excerpts from this text. Following the convention of arranging these in a narrative order that follows the broad storyline of the synoptic gospels produces this table of contents:

The disproportionate interest in the figure of John the Baptist may suggest that the *Gospel of the Ebionites* represented a close allegiance from members of the community who cherished this text towards the Baptist, whom they may have revered as some kind of foundational figure. There is emphasis placed on John's diet, with locusts being omitted from the description, which Epiphnius characterizes as a perversion of the gospel.

> And:

> 'It came to pass that John was baptizing; and there went out to him Pharisees and were baptized and all Jerusalem. And John had a garment of camel hair and a leather belt about his waist, and his food, as it says, was wild honey, the taste of which was that of manna, as a cake dipped in oil.'

> Thus they were resolved to pervert the word of truth into a lie and to put a cake in the place of locusts.

> (*Panarion* 30.13.4–5)

Similarly, it has Jesus deny that he wished to eat meat at the Passover. These features suggest that the Ebionites may have promoted a vegetarianism that is also evidenced in other branches of Christianity in the 2nd century.

The Jewish–Christian gospels perhaps stand closer to the canonical gospels than any of the other gospel-type texts that survive. Unfortunately, the fact that their preservation is refracted through the lenses of writers who are hostile to the perspectives that these texts promote means that ultimately the overall shape of their narratives and the details of the majority of the stories they contained are no longer recoverable.

The value of non-canonical gospels set during the life of Jesus

In many regards, the texts considered in this section are the most disparate and diverse. They are not unified by belonging to a common collection, or by presenting similar theological perspectives. Rather, the one common feature is that they purport to recount stories from the period of Jesus' public ministry – the same phase of Jesus' life that is the focus of the canonical gospels. Because of this overlap, comparisons may be made which allow for consideration of the possibility that these texts may preserve independent (perhaps earlier) versions of traditions that are paralleled in the four canonical gospels, or potentially they may offer that 'pearl of great price' – an authentic saying or incident from the life of Jesus otherwise unattested in the canonical sources.

Although this aspirational hope has motivated much interest in these texts, close analysis has shown that for the large part they appear to be later than the canonical gospels, they tend to draw upon the traditions embedded in those texts, and the new details they present are novelistic or fanciful. What then is the value of these texts that promised so much but delivered so little in scholarly attempts to learn more about the historical Jesus? First, it needs to be appreciated that these texts provide a glimpse into the way 2nd-century Christians handled and modified traditions concerning Jesus. Second, they highlight a number of pertinent issues for certain Christian groups: law-observance, vilifying Jews, heightening miraculous claims, and so on. Third, they reveal the textual nature of the preservation of early Christian tradition: with amateur scribes compiling their own collections of texts; the way Christians become innovators in using the new technology of the codex; and how they generated their own system of abbreviations. The dynamism and diversity of early Christianity comes to life through these texts, and the myth of a monolithic Christian movement existing in the 2nd and 3rd centuries is exploded.

Chapter 5

Secret revelations and dialogue gospels

Listening to Jesus beyond the grave

While travelling along the Damascus Road, Paul – or, as he was then, Saul – had a dramatic encounter that was to transform him from being a persecutor of the early movement centred on devotion to Jesus into a promoter and advocate for that system of faith. What changed him? The debate is endless and the attempts to psychologize the inner turmoil that led to this transformation tend to be pure speculation. The only firsthand data are Paul's own testimony and interpretation of events: that the God who had set him apart even from his mother's womb, called Paul on the Damascus Road through a revelation of Jesus his son given to Paul, in order that he might preach Jesus to the Gentiles (Gal. 1.15–16). For Paul, both the authority and authenticity of that revelatory calling was unquestionable. It transformed his understanding of the movement he had been persecuting and it shaped the events of the rest of his life. There was no division between the authority contained in what Jesus said during his earthly life and what he continued to say after his death. For Paul, both were undeniably authentic, and no separation was possible.

Yet, this raises the fundamental question that links both authority claims and decisions about legitimate interpretation: namely, what was to stop other believers receiving equally valid communications from the risen Jesus, and how could fellow believers question the veracity of such revelations if the recipient claimed they came directly from Jesus? Paul's call to preach to the Gentiles was a radical departure for a movement that had grown up inside Judaism as a messianic group. However, his 'revelation' appeared to be vindicated by the success he achieved among those non-Jewish believers who came to faith in Jesus. What other radical new teachings might the risen Jesus wish to communicate through later generations of followers? Some of the earliest surviving examples of this phenomenon from the post-Pauline phase can be seen in the gospel-like texts that record revelatory dialogues with Jesus, often in his risen state. The tone of these documents ranges from relatively sober and understandable encounters to the communication of bizarre descriptions of the aeons and cosmic realms – but they all claim to be written with the authority of Jesus behind them.

The *Gospel of Judas*

Exciting stories of the discovery of non-canonical gospel texts are not confined to the end of the 19th century. In fact, in many ways the most bizarre and tragic story belongs to the end of the 20th and start of the 21st centuries. It appears that four codices were 'discovered' (if that is not too soft a euphemism for what was probably tomb robbery) around 1978 near the village of Ambar, 60 kilometres north of Al Minya in Egypt. Details of the codices are still emerging but they seem to have comprised of the following: a Greek version of the Exodus, a Coptic version of Paul's epistles, a mathematical treatise, and a codex with multiple texts, the third of which was titled the *Gospel of Judas*.

The 'journey' of this final codex from discovery to publication has been extremely turbulent. It was left unstudied and decaying for several decades. The reason for the delay was simply the greed of those trying to sell the codex. The brittle, though at this stage well-preserved, codex came into the hands of an Egyptian antiquities dealer called Hanna. The story becomes somewhat murky at this point. Around 1980, Hanna attempted to sell a number of his sequestered treasures including the ancient codex. He arranged a viewing of the artefacts for a potential buyer, Nicolas Koutoulakis of Geneva, accompanied by two women. The day after the viewing, Hanna's apartment was robbed and all his antiquities taken. One of the women, described as a 'red-haired beauty' known as Mia, appears to have had some part in the robbery, since later the missing items were recovered indirectly from her. By 1982, the manuscript was back in Hanna's possession but now housed in a bank vault in Geneva. In 1983, a team of American scholars were allowed to view the codex for the purpose of purchasing it. They expected to have to pay in the region of $50,000 to $100,000, but they were astounded when Hanna asked for $3 millon. Negotiations broke down. The following year Hanna visited the United States with the codex, in an attempt to find a buyer. For safekeeping, the codex was deposited in a safe-deposit box in the Hicksville branch of Citibank on Long Island, New York. The manuscript was to languish in that bank vault for 16 years, undergoing serious disintegration in the humid atmosphere. On 3 April 2000, the codex was sold to Frieda Tchacos Nussberger, from whom the codex received its name – Codex Tchacos. It was then sold on to Bruce Ferrini, who appears to have frozen the manuscript in the belief that this would aid its preservation. Nothing could have been further from the truth. Freezing resulted in the partial destruction of the sap holding the fibres together, and accelerated the destruction and crumbling of the papyrus. When he was unable to pay the agreed cost of the codex, Ferrini returned it to Nussberger, although it appears that he held back some of the now highly fragmented pages.

In 2001, contact was made with the Maecenas Foundation in Basel, Switzerland. At last the work of serious reconstruction was to begin. Professional papyrologists described the codex as being the most structurally compromised they had ever seen. The work of reconstruction should be highly praised for its skill, care, and brilliant dedication to detail. Obviously gaps exist in the reconstruction, but large sections of the text were able to be preserved and the ordering was assisted by the presence of page numbers throughout the codex. The existence of the text of the *Gospel of Judas* was announced at the Eighth Congress of the International Association for Coptic Studies in Paris on 1 July 2004. The wider public dissemination of knowledge about the *Gospel of Judas* came through the May 2006 edition of *National Geographic* with the broadcast of an accompanying, although at times somewhat sensationalized, documentary. Approximately 28 years after discovery, the *Gospel of Judas* was finally in the public domain.

The actual contents of Codex Tchacos in its original form as unearthed in 1978 still are not totally certain. The codex certainly housed four texts, and it is likely that a fifth text was also originally part of the collection. The contents may be listed as follows:

TITLE PAGES	
The Letter of Peter to Philip	1–9
First Revelation of James	11–30
The Gospel of Judas	33–58
A Book of Allogenes	59–66
Corpus Hermeticum XIII	??

The fourth text is extremely fragmentary, it is impossible to determine if page 66 represents its conclusion or whether the text breaks off at some midpoint. Some of the fragments held by Ferrini, known as the Ohio fragments, have been identified with the *Corpus Hermeticum*. The recent critical edition of *The Gospel of Judas* published by *National Geographic* makes the following statement: the 'identification of the contents of Ohio 4578 is clear, and it suggests that Codex Tchacos originally also contained a hitherto unattested Coptic translation of *Corpus Hermeticum* XIII'. This description of contents reveals the literary tastes of the compiler of the codex, and one can note that he read an eclectic range of texts that can loosely be classified as 'Gnostic', and it is within this setting that the *Gospel of Judas* is to be understood.

Prior to the discovery of the text of the *Gospel of Judas*, its existence in antiquity was known by reference to its title. Originally written in Greek, Irenaeus states that:

> Others again declare that Cain derived his being from the Power above, and acknowledge that Esau, Korah, the Sodomites, and all such persons, are related to themselves. On this account, they add, they have been assailed by the Creator, yet no one of them has suffered injury. For Sophia was in the habit of carrying off that which belonged to her from them to herself. They declare that Judas the traitor was thoroughly acquainted with these things, and that he alone, knowing the truth as no others did, accomplished the mystery of the betrayal; by him all things, both earthly and heavenly, were thus thrown into confusion. They produce a fictitious history of this kind, which they style the Gospel of Judas.
>
> (Irenaeus, *Adversus Haereses* 1.31.1)

The *Gospel of Judas* represents a tractate from the Sethian branch of Gnosticism, and it purports to be a secret revelation of a conversation between Jesus and Judas that occurred three days before Jesus' final Passover. In this belief system, the divine unassailable God exists beyond the reach of the base material realm. From his mind comes forth his 'first-thought', a feminine deity called Barbelo, and in turn from her emanates her son Autogenes – the self-begotten one. After various stages of emanations, heavenly Seth, the perfect man, comes forth and his seed is the souls of repentant humanity. An abridged version of this cosmological salvation myth occurs in the *Gospel of Judas* (47.1–54.12) and it is this understanding that shapes the thought-world of the text.

One of the key concerns in the *Gospel of Judas* is to present a new understanding of the eponymous figure of Judas. While the original team of scholars deserve praise for their work of reconstructing the text, in the areas of translation and interpretation there were a number of fundamental errors. A leading scholar, April DeConick, has corrected the translation at a number of points and as a result has made the text more self-coherent and understandable as a Sethian parody of apostolic Christianity. Perhaps the most important case of mistranslation, which affects the way one understands the whole text, is to be found in *Gos. Jud.* 44.18–21. The translation published in the *National Geographic* edition reads as follows: 'When Jesus heard this, he laughed and said to him, "You thirteenth spirit, why do you try so hard? But speak up, and I shall bear with you." ' The trouble stems from the decision to render the Coptic loanword *daimon* as 'spirit' and not as 'demon'. While the translation of the term as 'spirit' is possible in Classical Greek from about five centuries before the composition of the text, close study of the use of the term in Gnostic texts from Nag Hammadi reveals that it uniformly is a negative reference denoting 'demons', 'devils', or 'evil spirits'. The original translation also presented Judas as occupying a privileged place in Jesus' eyes:

> When he heard this, Judas said to him, 'What good is it that I have received it? For you have set me apart for that generation.' Jesus answered and said, 'You will become the thirteenth, and you will be cursed by the other generations – and you will come to rule over them. In the last days they will curse your ascent to the holy generation.'
>
> (*Gos. Jud.* 46.14–47.1)

Yet a more accurate translation reveals that Judas is not set apart 'for' that generation, rather he is set apart 'from' it. This means that Judas is not set apart for the privileged Gnostic generation but he is separated from it – this is the very opposite of privilege.

Judas has insights into Jesus' origin that evade the other disciples, for he alone perceives that Jesus is 'from the immortal realm of

Barbelo' (*Gos. Jud.* 35.17–18). While Jesus acknowledges the superiority of Judas' insight in comparison to the rest of the disciples, he also gives this praise with a barbed warning: 'for somebody else will replace you in order that the twelve may again come to completion with their god' (*Gos. Jud.* 36.1–4).

Perhaps the most sensational aspect of the *Gospel of Judas* was seen as being the praise that Jesus supposedly lavishes upon Judas for his impending act of betrayal. The *National Geographic* translation states: 'But you will exceed all of them. For you will sacrifice the man that clothes me' (*Gos. Jud.* 56.17–18). Again, mistranslation and misunderstanding have led to seeing this as a request from Jesus to Judas that the latter might hand the former over to execution. There is no doubt a docetic perspective here which sees a separation between the spiritual 'ungenerated one' and the human outer shell, but there is no request for Judas to be the mechanism for the shedding of that shell. This verse needs to be read in the wider context where Jesus berates the other disciples for offering sacrifices to the lower god (*Gos. Jud.* 37.20–40.26), and where he commands them to stop sacrificing (*Gos. Jud.* 41.1–2). Yet Judas will do 'more than' these disciples who lack insight, he will actually sacrifice 'the man that clothes' Jesus. This is not a good thing, but it is a greater travesty. In effect, the text mocks apostolic Christianity by saying that even Judas the thirteenth demon had more insight concerning the origin of Jesus than the other disciples. Nonetheless, Judas perpetrated the worst sacrifice by handing Jesus over to death and the followers of the apostles venerate Jesus' death as an act of salvation when it was brought about by a demon. This bitter satire of apostolic Christianity may have been an attempt to win over converts, or it may have been written for the internal consumption of those already committed to Sethian beliefs. Either way, it is illustrative of the factionalism that existed in emergent Christianity and of the vastly different understandings of salvation and the nature of Jesus.

The *Gospel of Mary*

Fragments of the *Gospel of Mary* survive in three different manuscripts, two Greek and one Coptic. The Greek fragments are significantly earlier than the Coptic and it is generally agreed that the text was originally composed in Greek. The earliest fragment is probably Rylands Papyrus (P.Rhy.) 463. This is dated to around the early 3rd century and is a single-leaf text written on both sides, thus indicating that it probably came from a codex. The material contained by P.Rhy. 463 overlaps with the section numbered 17.4–19.5 in the more extensive Coptic text. The second, perhaps slightly later, Greek fragment was discovered at Oxyrhynchus (P.Oxy. 3525) and published in 1983. This papyrus scrap has text only on one side, thus suggesting it was written in scroll format. It also overlaps entirely with the Coptic text for the material in 9.1–10.14.

The fullest witness to the *Gospel of Mary* is a Coptic translation, purchased in 1896 by Carl Reinhardt from a dealer in Cairo, which has been dated to the 5th century. This copy is, however, incomplete. The page numbering suggests that the text occupied the first 19 pages of the codex, of which only pages 7–10 and 15–19 survive. The end of the text is clearly present on page 19, so the ending is certain, but although likely, it is impossible to be sure that this text commenced on page 1 of the codex. The dating of the composition of the text is uncertain. It must be placed before the surviving Greek fragments, which themselves date from around the early 3rd century. It does not reflect some of the more developed mystical soteriological systems of Gnostic texts known by Irenaeus, who wrote around AD 180. The text also appears to show knowledge of the canonical gospels, so it must be later than the 1st century. Perhaps the most likely date range is some point within 25 years either side of AD 150, i.e. AD 125–175. Publication of the Coptic papyrus was greatly delayed; the tragedy of a burst water main in a printing house in Leipzig in 1912 meant that the originally prepared edition of the text was destroyed before going to press in 1912. The intervention of two world wars delayed publication further until the text was finally printed in 1955.

Contents

The text falls into two main sections, with a bridging framework between that links the two major parts. This apparent editorial framework also resurfaces at the end of the text. First, there is a dialogue between the risen Jesus and his disciples (7.1–9.5). This ends with a note of the risen saviour's departure from the disciples followed by the introduction of Mary Magdalene (9.5–10.9). The remaining text preserves Mary Magdalene's report of a vision she had of the Lord (10.10–23; 15.1–17.9) and the ensuing debate between Mary and three other disciples about the validity of her vision (17.10–19.5).

The opening section is wide-ranging, but contains a clear cosmological focus. It discusses the nature and the conservation or destruction of matter, the origin of sin, and the appearance of 'the Good' as a restorative force. This is followed by a call to obedience, and a series of sayings from the risen Jesus that are reminiscent of material in the canonical accounts, that commend peace, warn against straying from the teachings of Jesus, caution against false claims of the Son of Man's return, promise that seekers will find him, command the preaching of the gospel, and prohibit the introduction of any rules beyond those given by Jesus, especially 'laws' like those given by the 'law-giver'. This dialogue could be responding to a number of ecclesial situations around the middle of the 2nd century. There could be disquiet over developing hierarchical forms of church leadership, especially with standardization of practice. The last concern over promoting laws like those given by Moses may also be a reference to Jewish–Christian groups advocating adherence to the Jewish law. The exact situation against which these injunctions might be warning is uncertain, but the spirit of the dialogue is to uphold variety and to guard against an overly structured form of discipleship.

The transitional material contained in *Gos. Mary* 9.5–10.9 serves to introduce a new dynamic in the text. Upon the departure of Jesus, the disciples weep and wonder out loud how they will preach the gospel to the Gentiles since they did not spare Jesus. Unlike certain non-canonical gospels that shift the blame for the death of Jesus on to the Jews, this text sees the Gentiles as responsible for his death. In response to the grief of the disciples, Mary (not previously mentioned in the extant portion of the text) arises and greets them. After comforting the disciples, it is stated that: 'When Mary said these things, she turned their hearts to the Good, and they began to discuss the words of the Saviour' (*Gos. Mary* 9.21–24). Before Mary launches into her speech, Peter addresses her, revealing two important perspectives. First, it is acknowledged by Peter himself that 'the Saviour loved you more than the rest of women', and second, that she is the possessor of knowledge of hidden sayings of the Saviour which were not disclosed to the disciples: 'Tell us the words of the Saviour which you remember, which you know but we do not, and which we have not heard' (*Gos. Mary* 10.4–6). Thus the narrative is set up to introduce the report of Mary's visionary conversation with the Lord, having acknowledged the legitimacy of this vision through the apostolic authority of Peter.

The opening section of the reported vision is brief, caused by the large lacuna in the text of four missing pages. It does discuss the medium through which visions occur. In response to Mary's question, the Saviour answers that the one who sees a vision 'does not see through the soul, nor through the spirit, but the mind which is between the two sees the vision and it . . .' (*Gos. Mary* 10.20–24). When the text resumes, it is in the middle of a discussion about 'powers'. The soul, presumably of some representative believer, is engaged on a journey through the realms of the spheres occupied by these powers. Here 'desire' is being discussed as the second in a list of four powers. 'Desire' is personified and is in conversation with 'the soul'. Acknowledging that 'desire' considers the soul as only a garment, the soul departs from the presence of 'desire'. Next it encounters the third power – 'ignorance'. The primary fault of 'ignorance' is that it passes judgement without understanding. The soul admits that previously it was bound, although it did not itself bind anybody. This may resonate with the warning in the first section not to 'give a law like the law-giver lest you be bound by it' (*Gos. Mary* 9.3–4). Upon overcoming the third power, the soul continues its upward journey, coming into contact with the fourth power – which, although not initially named, appears like some multi-headed hydra, having seven forms. These forms are named as darkness, desire, ignorance, jealousy of death, the kingdom of the flesh, foolish understanding, and wrathful wisdom. It is only after this description of the seven forms that the text states that 'these are the seven powers of Wrath' (*Gos. Mary* 16.12–13). Thus it appears that the climactic fourth power is 'wrath', but this subdivides into seven entities which are themselves designated as powers.

Such fragmentation of entities is a common feature of Gnostic cosmologies, often with certain pieces of a higher-order being falling to a lower realm and resulting in a more derivative and partial mode of existence. It is interesting that the second and third forms of the fourth power, 'wrath', are the same entities that are described as the second and third powers in their own right, namely 'desire' and 'ignorance'. If this pattern holds, then the first power, which presumably was mentioned on the missing pages of the text, could likely have been 'darkness'. The soul responds to 'wrath' that it has gained release from the world and from henceforth it will reside in 'the rest of the time of the season of the aeon in silence' (*Gos. Mary* 17.5–7). Having outlined the escape and restoration of the soul from the various powers, Mary's vision ends, and as if to underline the purity and insight of her own soul, she falls silent.

The response of the named disciples to Mary's vision may symbolically represent the reaction of apostolic Christianity to mystical branches of the movement. Andrew declares that he is unconvinced by Mary's visionary account.

> But Andrew answered and said to the brethren, 'Say what you wish to say about what she has said. I myself do not believe that the Saviour said this. For these teachings seem to be giving different ideas'. Peter answered and spoke about the same things. He asked them about the Saviour: 'He did not speak with a women without our knowing, and not openly did he? Shall we turn around and all listen to her? Did he prefer her to us?'
>
> (*Gos. Mary* 19.10–22)

As in the *Gospel of Thomas* and the *Gospel of Philip*, here also Mary Magdalene is presented as a figure of resistance against apostolic Christianity, especially in the form represented by Peter and other named apostles. She seems to offer an alternative kind of authority stream, and therefore is claimed as a valid source of tradition that stems back to the risen Jesus. The portraits of both Peter and Andrew are used to subvert the authority structures that claim to be derived from these figures in the 2nd-century Church. Mary's reaction is that of an aggrieved and grieving individual, who cannot believe that the validity of her vision of the Saviour has not been accepted: 'My brother Peter, what do you think? Do you think that I thought this up in my heart, or that I am lying about the Saviour?' (*Gos. Mary* 18.2–5). The next figure to appear in the narrative is a certain Levi, whose status is not explained, although he appears to be one of the disciples of Jesus. He may be understood as the same person who is mentioned in the two accounts of the tax-collector Levi who is called to follow Jesus (Mark 2.13–17 and Luke 5.27–32). Levi takes a mediating position, although he is more clearly convinced by Mary's vision. He accuses Peter of 'hot-headedness', and acknowledges that the Saviour did indeed love Mary more than the disciples. Levi counsels that rather than engage in bickering, they should 'put on the perfect man' in order that they might 'preach the gospel, not laying down any other rule or law beyond what the Saviour said' (*Gos. Mary* 18.18–21). The narrative ends with the disciples going out to preach in accordance with Levi's injunction. Finally, the title of the document is written at the end in Coptic: 'The gospel according to Mary.'

Purpose

What is to be made of this complex text? The clear difference in tone between the first and second major section, the dialogue between the risen Jesus and his disciples (7.1–9.5) and the account of Mary's vision (10.10–23; 15.1–17.9) has led to the suggestion that the text as it is preserved is a composite which knits together two originally discrete documents. The character of the vision is very different to the dialogue, and Mary plays no part in the opening section. While not minimizing these highly significant differences or necessarily wishing to exclude the theory of a composite text, it can be noted that there are certain affinities in both of the large sections, especially in terms of not being bound by either legalistic perspectives (9.4), nor allowing the soul to be bound by the powers (16.17). This may suggest that it is not impossible to maintain that the text may have been written as a unified composition.

Peter's attack on Mary is framed in terms of her womanhood. This has led to the suggestion that the text is an intentional tool of feminist resistance. While such a womanist perspective has been theologically appealing in some quarters, it is uncertain whether the text will actually bear the weight of this agenda. First, Andrew's attack against Mary's teaching is not gender-related, but stems from the different quality of her teaching. Although Peter may speak with the androcentric perspective of his time, his primary concern is said to be the same as that of Andrew, namely the source of this previously undisclosed teaching. Second, if Mary's gender were the issue in relation to her status among the apostles, it is strange that the text keeps her voiceless and instead

129

allows Levi to present her defence. This is surely not the vehicle of feminist resistance. Rather, the issue appears not to be that of gender or the status of individual figures; instead the text promotes the status of secret or personal revelations which seem to add new elements to the received tradition. It appears that in many ways the ancient question the *Gospel of Mary* was seeking to address was similar to the one that has been the basis of much of the discussion throughout this book: namely, what is the 'gospel' and how are the boundaries of that category established?

Nonetheless, the *Gospel of Mary* does not represent a totally closed division between apostolic Christianity and the mystical type of belief promoted in Mary's vision. This may provide evidence for seeing this text written at an early stage of the dispute between these opposing views, when there was still hope of a rapprochement of the type advocated by the literary figure of Levi. Thus, perhaps more than any other of the non-canonical gospels, the *Gospel of Mary* may allow one to more fully appreciate what lay at the heart of the division between emergent orthodox Christianity and developing Gnostic versions of that faith. Specifically, the difficulty was the validity of ongoing visionary encounters with the risen Jesus, and the problems of accommodating such new perspectives within existing understandings of faith. For the traditionalists, the core of the Christian faith had been fixed by the apostolic traditions received and transmitted through recognized significant authority figures. However, for Gnostic believers, visions could be received by any soul that was seeking escape from the constraining powers of the physical universe.

The significance of secret revelations and dialogue gospels

Sociologists of new religious movements in the 20th and 21st centuries have highlighted the spread and appeal of charismatic forms of belief, which promise direct unmediated access to the divine. Personal search and personal journey are important aspects, albeit within the context of a community of like-minded co-religionists. The opportunities for creativity and spontaneous expression of religious fervour freed from the fixity of liturgical forms and the rigidity of hierarchies has resonated with many who feel alienated by institutional religion. Although still a relatively new phenomenon, by the 2nd century Christianity had formed many settled structures, it was developing standardized patterns of worship and had begun to regulate its leadership around a local bishop. This tendency to 'routinize the charisma', as it is described in scholarly literature, may have been necessary for the long-term survival of the movement as an empire-wide phenomenon. However, it also left many feeling alienated and hankering after the golden age when the Jesus movement provided a close-knit familial community. In its place they may have felt the early Church was evolving into a somewhat colder and autocratically regulated belief system. Both to resist these developments and to legitimize one's own desires, visions received directly from the Saviour allowed for the creation of the space in which to practise the type of religion that permitted a more direct encounter with the divine and a more active participation in the quest for personal salvation. The gospel-like texts that gave insights through communication with the risen Jesus were products of this larger spiritual impulse.

Chapter 6
Insights from the non-canonical gospels

What is a 'non-canonical' gospel?

In the introductory chapter the question was raised concerning what the terms 'non-canonical' and 'gospel' actually denoted. Hesitant answers were provided. After considering various non-canonical gospels, those answers have probably not become any less hesitant, but perhaps the reasons for hesitancy have become clearer. The range of texts to which both ancient and modern scholars have attached the label 'gospel' is in some ways amazing. Starting with the four canonical gospels, while Matthew, Mark, and Luke are extremely similar, no doubt due to the literary dependence between these texts, the fourth gospel, John's account, already shows a diversity of form, language, and theology. Yet these differences appear relatively minor when compared with other writings outside the confines of these four canonical texts. Perhaps those texts that cover the same phase of Jesus' life as the canonical accounts show the most commonality with the four gospels of the New Testament. Thus the *Gospel of Peter* or the fragmentary stories in Papyrus Oxyrhynchus 840 and Papyrus Egerton 2 appear to cohere with familiar accounts of Jesus' life. While such texts are easier to appropriate under the title of 'gospel', this does not say anything about their authenticity, nor does it automatically support claims that they may be a repository of alternative traditions about Jesus. Rather, with the three non-canonical texts mentioned above, it was argued that in different ways they were all derivative upon the New Testament gospels and that they probably preserved little if any independent historical details that could be traced back to the historical Jesus.

Similarly, the infancy gospels only further problematize the understanding of the category of 'gospel'. These were seen as being essentially gap-filling exercises which sought to satisfy the curiosity of the pious. Yet even texts as bizarre as the *Infancy Gospel of Thomas* with its maverick and deadly boy-Jesus could be labelled as a 'gospel'. The *Protevangelium of James* circulated in antiquity without the term 'gospel' being attached. That categorization was applied by its modern rediscoverer. Nag Hammadi texts differed greatly in form and content, yet four of the texts in that collection bear the term 'gospel' in their titles. One of these, the *Gospel of Thomas*, is the least speculative among this group of texts. Yet it is different to the narrative-type gospels in that it consists of a series of 114 sayings which seem to have little structural organization beyond being a compendium of words of Jesus. With the other Nag Hammadi gospels one enters into a different world of theology and thought. This combined with the variations in literary genre makes one realize how stretched the term 'gospel' had become. Therefore, perhaps the most that can be concluded is that texts which appear to have some link with Jesus and also relate an understanding of 'good news' or salvation, seem to have had the potential to be classified as gospels.

The category of 'non-canonical' is at one level much easier, since by definition it describes any text not in the canon of the New Testament. However, the foregoing discussion of specific texts demonstrated that the distinction is perhaps not simple. When considering the *Protevangelium of James*, it was noted that this was a widely circulating text, which in the Greek-speaking church was generally regarded as being 'orthodox' in its theological outlook and hence was used to supplement mainstream beliefs. Others regarded the theological value of this text as virtually nil – from such a perspective the text was deemed to be non-canonical. Thus the classification of a text as being 'canonical' presses one to ask the question, 'canonical for whom?' The Nag Hammadi library represents a highly varied collection of manuscripts, yet this corpus of texts may well have functioned as an authoritative collection for the readers of those texts – or was it no more than a chance miscellany of literary works? Therefore the classification of texts as 'canonical' or 'non-canonical' is an arbitrary and perspectival choice. Perhaps the best reason for retaining the distinction is simply that it preserves the traditional categories and thus it can be employed for ease of reference.

The non-canonical gospels and the historical Jesus

Conspiracy theorists seem to adore the non-canonical gospels. They are employed to support the suggestion that the image of the true Jesus has been suppressed, buried under layers of ecclesiastical constructs that domesticate the revolutionary message of the teacher from Nazareth. It is true that by comparison the canonical accounts present a relatively tame picture of Jesus, who is best understood within a 1st-century Jewish context. Perhaps it is because the canonical gospels present a Jesus whose teaching and life is tightly linked to a specific historical setting that in some ways these texts have become less attractive to postmodern tastes. By contrast, the non-canonical accounts are often free from the limitation of historical context, and their esoteric teachings are ambiguous enough to be interpreted in multiple ways. Yet even if the utility of the ideas in non-canonical gospels is more appealing for those pursuing contemporary spiritualities, this does not make their portrait of Jesus more authentically historical. If Jesus, the 1st-century Galilean, has become irrelevant to modern minds, he cannot be reclaimed by privileging historically dubious representations of him. Bad history does not make for good faith. It needs to be acknowledged that most of the non-canonical texts appear either to derive in various ways from the four gospels of the New Testament, or they seem to be the products of speculative and visionary theological schools that flourished between the 2nd and 4th centuries.

This is not to say that no material in the non-canonical gospels has any claim of originating with the historical Jesus. Rather, expectations should be limited. As has been discussed, the *Gospel of Thomas* is the most likely source of extra-biblical authentic Jesus tradition being preserved among the non-canonical gospels. Some forms of sayings which parallel canonical versions actually appear more primitive and consequently raise the possibility that they retain a form of wording closer to that actually spoken by Jesus. Again there is still a huge gap between what is recorded and what Jesus may actually have said. The *Gospel of Thomas*, at least in the fullest form in which it is preserved, is written in Coptic. This is likely to be a translation of a Greek version, evidenced by the fragments discovered at Oxyrhynchus. Jesus himself almost certainly gave his teaching in Aramaic. So even if the *Gospel of Thomas* does preserve the wording of a saying closer to that uttered by the historical Jesus than a version preserved in the New Testament, this is still perhaps two stages of translation removed from Jesus' actual spoken words. Where the *Gospel of Thomas* may provide more interesting data is when it presents otherwise unattested sayings that have a degree of probability of originating with Jesus. In reality, most scholars who even entertain this possibility would place only a small selection of sayings from *Thomas* in this category.

Belief that the non-canonical gospels offer the possibility of repristinating early Christianity is just that – a belief! When the material contained in these texts is analysed from a thoroughgoing historical perspective, the vast majority of sayings and narratives are seen to stem from the period subsequent to the New Testament and thus have lesser claim than the canonical gospels to be accurate portraits of the historical Jesus. Does this then mean that the study of non-canonical gospels is a fruitless endeavour?

Hopefully not, but it needs to be recognized that their value lies elsewhere.

What is the value of the non-canonical gospels?

Hopefully by now it will be recognized that texts can have multiple layers of historical contexts. A modern historical novel, set in Tudor England say, may wish to transport readers back to that period, or help them to experience the authentic feel of Elizabethan England. Attention may be given to dress, diet, and even details of the station and influence of major figures. Yet often, in order to connect with a modern readership contemporary concerns must be projected back on to ancient characters. Thus the psychological, relational, and financial concerns they express can have a very modern feel, which while resonating with 21st-century readers would nonetheless actually be foreign to the purported context.

The same is true with the majority of non-canonical gospels. They reflect the concerns of their world more closely than the world of the 1st-century Jesus. Yet for the historian of ancient Christianity this is itself an extremely important window onto the piety, practices, and beliefs of diverse groups of Christians in the 2nd and 3rd centuries – and beyond. For example, the *Gospel of Peter* shifts the blame for the crucifixion heavily onto the Jews and seeks to absolve the Roman authorities. This does not mean that its storyline accurately represents the 1st-century historical reality. However, it is vitally important to understand that at least by the end of the 2nd century, early Christians were downplaying Roman involvement, perhaps to remove the offence of Jesus having been crucified by imperial authority, and simultaneously allowing Christians to scapegoat one of the groups that most fiercely disputed claims of Jesus' messiahship and divinity.

Non-canonical gospels are also a powerful witness to the diversity of early Christianity itself. It has long been recognized that 'the winners write history'. Even within Christianity there have been victors and those whose perspectives have been defeated and rejected. Regardless of whether this is piously seen as being due to divine providence, or rather more pragmatically as being due to the vagaries of history, it remains the case that what emerged as 'orthodox' Christianity was able to produce the narrative of the history of the church. In so doing, it either neglected competing understandings of the faith, or represented these as heretical and deviant. More than anything else, what the non-canonical gospels permit is the opportunity to hear once again those voices from the margins. By reading these texts it is possible to enter the thought-world of various mystical and experiential forms of Christianity. The discovery of such texts has rescued long-lost voices and in the process enlarged the understanding of the diversity and variety of early Christianity.

Further reading

Collections of Texts

J. K. Elliott, *The Apocryphal New Testament* (Oxford: Clarendon Press, 1993; first paperback edition 2005).

This is the most accessible and fullest one-volume collection of non-canonical New Testament texts.

E. Hennecke and W. Schneemelcher (eds.), *New Testament Apocrypha*, Volume One: *Gospels and Related Writings*; Volume Two: *Writings Relating to the Apostles; Apocalypses and Related Subjects*, rev. edn. (R. McL. Wilson, trans.; Louisville, KY: Westminster John Knox Press, 1991, 1993).

A translation into English of the standard German reference work. This is in the process of being fully revised and rewritten for a new edition.

J. M. Robinson (ed.), *The Nag Hammadi Library in English*, rev. edn. (Leiden: Brill, 1996).

This is the standard one-volume English translation of the Nag Hammadi texts.

A. E. Barnard, *Other Early Christian Gospels: A Critical Edition of the Surviving Greek Manuscripts* (LNTS 315; London: T&T Clark, 2006).

A collection of images, transcriptions, and translations of fragmentary Greek non-canonical gospel texts.

Online Resources

Useful websites include:
http://www.gnosis.org/naghamm/nhl.html

http://www.nag-hammadi.com/
http://www-user.uni-bremen.de/~wie/Egerton/Egerton_home.html
http://forbiddengospels.blogspot.com/
http://wesley.nnu.edu/Biblical_Studies/noncanon/gospels.htm

Treatments of Collections of Non-Canonical Texts

D. R. Cartlidge and J. K. Elliott, *Art and the Christian Apocrypha*
(London/New York: Routledge, 2001).

J. D. Crossan, *Four Other Gospels: Shadows on the Contours of Canon*
(Minneapolis, MN: Winston Press, 1985).

B. Ehrman, *Lost Christianities: The Battles for Scripture and the Faiths
We Never Knew* (Oxford: Oxford University Press, 2003).

J. K. Elliott, *A Synopsis of the Apocryphal Nativity and Infancy
Narratives* (NTTS 34; Leiden: Brill, 2006).

P. Foster (ed.), *The Non-Canonical Gospels* (London: T&T Clark, 2008).

P. Jenkins, *Hidden Gospels: How the Search for Jesus Lost Its Way*
(Oxford: Oxford University Press, 2001).

H.-J. Klauck, *Apocryphal Gospels: An Introduction* (Eng. trans.;
London: T&T Clark, 2003).

H. Koester, *Ancient Christian Gospels: Their History and Development*
(London/Philadelphia, PA: SCM/TPI, 1990).

F. Lapham, *An Introduction to the New Testament Apocrypha*
(London: T&T Clark, 2003).

J. D. Turner and A. McGuire (eds.), *The Nag Hammadi Library after
Fifty Years: Proceedings of the 1995 Society of Biblical Literature
Commemoration* (Leiden: Brill, 1997).

Works on Individual Non-Canonical Texts

H. I. Bell and T. C. Skeat, *Fragments of an Unknown Gospel and Other
Early Christian Papyri* (London: British Museum, 1935).

T. Chartrand-Burke, 'The *Infancy Gospel of Thomas*: The Text, its
Origins, and its Transmission' (Ph.D. diss., University of Toronto,
2001).

A. D. DeConick, *Recovering the Original Gospel of Thomas: A History of
the Gospel and Its Growth* (LNTS 286; London: T&T Clark, 2005).

—— *The Original Gospel of Thomas in Translation, with a
Commentary and New English Translation of the Complete Gospel*
(LNTS 287; London: T&T Clark, 2006).

—— *The Thirteenth Apostle: What the Gospel of Judas Really Says* (London: T&T Clark, 2007).

S. J. Gathercole, *The Gospel of Judas* (Oxford: Oxford University Press, 2007).

R. F. Hock, *The Infancy Gospels of James and Thomas* (Santa Rosa, CA: Polebridge Press, 1995).

K. L. King, *The Gospel of Mary of Magdala: Jesus and the First Woman Apostle* (Santa Rosa, CA: Polebridge Press, 2003).

T. J. Kraus, *Ad fontes: Original Manuscripts and Their Significance for Studying Early Christianity – Selected Essays* (Leiden: Brill, 2007).

M. J. Kruger, *The Gospel of the Saviour: An Analysis of P.Oxy. 840 and its Place in the Gospel Traditions of Early Christianity* (TENT 1; Leiden: Brill, 2005).

S. Patterson, *The Gospel of Thomas and Jesus* (Sonoma, CA: Polebridge Press, 1993).

C. M. Tuckett, *The Gospel of Mary* (Oxford: Oxford University Press, 2007).

M. L. Turner, *The Gospel According to Philip: The Sources and Coherence of an Early Christian Collection* (Leiden: Brill, 1996).

R. Uro, *Thomas: Seeking the Historical Context of the Gospel of Thomas* (London: T&T Clark, 2003).

R. Valantasis, *The Gospel of Thomas* (London/New York: Routledge, 1997).

R. McL. Wilson, *The Gospel of Philip* (London: A. R. Mowbray & Co., 1962).

Further reading

Works Providing Important Background to the Non-Canonical Gospels

R. E. Brown, *The Birth of the Messiah* (ABRL, rev. edn.; New York: Doubleday, 1993).

W. H. C. Frend, *The Rise of Christianity* (Philadelphia, PA: Fortress, 1984).

J. Jeremias, *Unknown Sayings of Jesus* (London: SCM, 1964).

A. H. B. Logan, *The Gnostics: Identifying an Early Christian Cult* (London: T&T Clark, 2006).

J. Robinson and H. Koester (eds.), *Trajectories through Early Christianity* (Philadelphia, PA: Fortress Press, 1971).

References

Chapter 1

The manuscript found in Archduke Rainer's collection is known as
the Fayyum Fragment and has been given the papyrus abbreviation
P.Vindob.G 2325. See the discussion of this manuscript by
T. J. Kraus, 'The Fayum Gospel', in P. Foster (ed.), *The Non-Canonical Gospels* (London: T&T Clark, 2008), pp. 150–6.

A fascinating discussion of the archaeology of the Oxyrhynchus site
and the significance of the papyrus documents unearthed there can
be found in P. Parsons, *City of the Sharp-Nosed Fish: Greek Lives in
Roman Egypt* (London: Weidenfeld and Nicolson, 2007).

N. T. Wright claims that the *Gospel of Judas* is not a true 'gospel' in his
Judas and the Gospel of Jesus (London: SPCK, 2006), pp. 27–39.

The evolution in meaning of the term 'gospel' is carefully traced by
G. N. Stanton, *Jesus and Gospel* (Cambridge: Cambridge University
Press, 2004), esp. chapter 2, pp. 9–62.

For the wider political situation in Rome in AD 69, see P. A. L.
Greenhalgh, *The Year of the Four Emperors* (London: Weidenfeld
and Nicolson, 1975).

Martin Hengel argues that the titles of the written gospels were not
added secondarily, but were part of the gospels as they originally
circulated. M. Hengel, *The Four Gospels and the One Gospel of
Jesus Christ* (London: SCM, 2000), pp. 50–3.

Irenaeus uses the notion of 'appropriateness' to justify why the number
of gospels can be no fewer or no more than four. See D. Minns,
'Irenaeus', *Expository Times* 120 (2009), pp. 157–166.

The estimate of about 40 known gospel-like texts is suggested in recent publications: C. M. Tuckett, 'Forty Other Gospels', in M. Bockmuehl and D. A. Hagner (eds.), *The Written Gospel* (Cambridge: Cambridge University Press, 2005), pp. 238–53; C. Hedrick, 'The 34 Gospels: Diversity and Division Among Earliest Christians', *Bible Review* 18.3 (2002): 20–31, 46–7.

The two most sustained challenges to the use of the whole category of 'Gnosticism' have come from M. A. Williams, *Rethinking 'Gnosticism': An Argument for Dismantling a Dubious Category* (Princeton: Princeton University Press, 1996) and K. L. King, *What is Gnosticism?* (Cambridge, MA: Harvard University Press, 2003).

For a defence of the retention of the term 'Gnostic', see A. H. B. Logan, *The Gnostics: Identifying an Early Christian Cult* (London: T&T Clark, 2006) and B. Pearson, *Ancient Gnosticism: Traditions and Literature* (Minneapolis: Fortress, 2007).

For a discussion of the succession lists of bishops of Rome being an artificial construct of the second half of the 2nd century, see P. Lampe, *From Paul to Valentinus: Christians at Rome in the First Two Centuries* (London: Continuum, 2003), pp. 404–6.

For an advanced discussion of Valentinism, see E. Thomassen, *The Spiritual Seed: The Church of the 'Valentinians'* (Leiden: Brill, 2006).

For the debate about Gnosticism before Christianity, see E. Yamauchi, 'The Issue of Pre-Christian Gnosticism Reviewed in the Light of the Nag Hammadi Texts', in J. D. Turner and A. McGuire (eds.), *The Nag Hammadi Library after Fifty Years: Proceedings of the 1995 Society of Biblical Literature Commemoration* (Leiden: Brill, 1997), pp. 72–88.

On the *Gospel of the Saviour*, see C. W. Hedrick and P. A. Mirecki, *Gospel of the Savior: A New Ancient Gospel* (Santa Rosa, CA: Polebridge Press, 1999).

The discovery of the *Gospel of Judas* was brought to wider public attention through a series of *National Geographic* publications and television documentaries. See *The National Geographic* (May 2006): 78–95.

Two mainstream treatments dealing with the methodological problems that attend historical Jesus research can be found in E. P. Sanders, *Jesus and Judaism* (London: SCM, 1985), and the multi-volume work of J. P. Meier, *A Marginal Jew: Rethinking the Historical Jesus*, 3 vols. (New York: Doubleday, 1991, 1994, 2001).

The classical critique of the view of Christianity as a unified religion was outlined in the 1930s, see W. Bauer, *Orthodoxy and Heresy in Earliest Christianity* (English translation, London: SCM, 1972; German original, 1934).

A radical redating of non-canonical gospel material can be seen in Appendix 1 of J. D. Crossan, *The Historical Jesus: The Life of a Mediterranean Jewish Peasant* (San Francisco: HarperCollins, 1992), pp. 427–34.

The colour-coded results of the Jesus Seminar were published in R. W. Funk and R. W. Hoover (eds.), *The Five Gospels: The Search for the Authentic Words of Jesus* (Toronto: Polebridge/Macmillan, 1993).

Chapter 2

The James Robinson quote is from his 'Nag Hammadi: The First Fifty Years', in J. D. Turner and A. McGuire (eds.), *The Nag Hammadi Library after Fifty Years: Proceedings of the 1995 Society of Biblical Literature Commemoration* (Leiden: Brill, 1997), pp. 3–6. See also J. M. Robinson (ed.), *The Nag Hammadi Library in English*, revised edn. (Leiden: Brill, 1996).

On the revelation dialogues, see K. L. King, *The Secret Revelation of John* (Cambridge, MA: Harvard University Press, 2006).

The English translations of the Coptic sayings are largely drawn from A. Guillaumont *et al.* (eds.), *The Gospel According to Thomas: Coptic Text Established and Translated*, revised edn. (Leiden: Brill, 1998), but other translations are consulted and the renderings offered here do not strictly follow any one translation. Also see the English translations in A. D. DeConick, *The Original Gospel of Thomas in Translation, with a Commentary and New English Translation of the Complete Gospel* (LNTS 287; London: T&T Clark, 2006).

For a discussion of the enigmatic Saying 42, see R. Valantasis, *The Gospel of Thomas* (London/New York: Routledge, 1997), p. 118. He notes that this saying is primarily about 'disengagement' and promotes 'the centrality of individual as distinct from group identity'.

On James the Just, see B. D. Chilton and C. A. Evans (eds.), *James the Just and Christian Origins* (Leiden: Brill, 1999).

For a discussion of the possibility that salvation was a two-stage process for women, see J. Buckley, 'An Interpretation of Logion 114 in *The*

Gospel of Thomas', *NovT* 27 (1985): 245–72. By contrast, DeConick suggests that 'gender refashioning for women would have stressed encratic behaviour, particularly celibacy and their refusal to bear children': *The Original Gospel of Thomas in Translation*, p. 297.

For a detailed discussion of the Valentinian perspectives in the *Gospel of Philip*, see M. L. Turner, *The Gospel of Philip: The Sources and Coherence of an Early Christian Collection* (Leiden: Brill, 1996).

The page-referencing system for the *Gospel of Philip* follows that adopted by Isenberg in his standard edition of the text.
W. W. Isenberg, 'Gospel According to Philip', in B. Layton (ed.), *Nag Hammadi Codex II*, pp. 2–7.

The English translation of the passage in the *Gospel of Philip* where Jesus kisses Mary is taken from the work of W. W. Isenberg, 'The Gospel of Philip (II,3)', and is most conveniently accessed in J. M. Robinson (ed.), *The Nag Hammadi Library in English*, revised edn. (Leiden: Brill, 1996), p. 148. The more sexualized version of this text is from R. McL. Wilson, *The Gospel of Philip* (London: Mowbray, 1962), p. 114. He helpfully brackets the reconstructed elements, and does not promote the speculative ideas that have often been built upon this text. Various Internet sites suggest the type of intimate relationship Jesus may have shared with Mary Magdalene.

For an important discussion of the term 'docetic', see M. Slusser, 'Docetism: A Historical Definition', *Second Century* 1.3 (1981): 163–72.

The translation of the passage about Jesus on the cross is taken from H. W. Attridge and G. W. MacRae, 'The Gospel of Truth (I,3 and XII,2)', in J. M. Robinson (ed.), *The Nag Hammadi Library in English*, revised edn. (Leiden: Brill, 1996), p. 42.

The phenomenon of overlapping topics treated by both Justin and Valentinian texts has been noted by P. Parvis, 'Justin, Philosopher and Martyr: The Posthumous Creation of the Second Apology', in S. Parvis and P. Foster (eds.), *Justin and His Worlds* (Minneapolis: Fortress, 2007), pp. 22–37, esp. 32–4.

On the *Gospel of the Egyptians*, see A. Böhlig and F. Wisse (eds.), *Nag Hammadi Codices III,2 and IV,2. The Gospel of the Egyptians (The Holy Book of the Great Invisible Spirit)* (Leiden: Brill, 1975). See also A. Böhlig and F. Wisse, 'The Gospel of the Egyptians (III,2 and IV,2)', in J. M. Robinson (ed.), *The Nag Hammadi Library in English*, revised edn. (Leiden: Brill, 1996), pp. 208–19.

The translation of the 'nonsense vowels' quote is taken from H. W. Attridge and G. W. MacRae, 'The Gospel of Truth (I,3 and XII,2)',

in J. M. Robinson (ed.), *The Nag Hammadi Library in English*,
revised edn. (Leiden: Brill, 1996), p. 42.

Chapter 3

The quotes about the childhood Jesus are from T. Chartrand-Burke,
'The Infancy Gospel of Thomas', in P. Foster (ed.), *The Non-
Canonical Gospels* (London: T&T Clark, 2008), p. 126.

Apart from the 4th-century Codex Sinaiticus recovered from the
monastery of St Catherine at Mount Sinai, Constantin von
Tischendorf also deciphered the palimpsest Codex Ephraemi
Rescriptus, and published a critical edition of Codex
Claromontanus containing the Pauline epistles. He was also active
in publishing texts that now constitute the New Testament
apocrypha: *De Evangeliorum apocryphorum origine et usu* (1851);
Acta Apostolorum apocrypha (1851); *Evangelia apocrypha* (1853;
2nd edn., 1876); *Apocalypses apocryphae* (1866).

The English translations in this chapter of both the *Infancy Gospel
of Thomas* and the *Protevangelium of James* are largely drawn from
R. F. Hock, *The Infancy Gospels of James and Thomas* (Santa Rosa,
CA: Polebridge, 1995). At a few points modifications are made
based on a more exact translation of the Greek text. In particular,
the translation 'sodomite, ungodly and ignorant...' more
accurately represents the wording of the Greek text than Hock's
somewhat 'domesticated' translation 'Damn you, you irreverent
fool!' (It is difficult to determine whether in this context the term
'sodomite' has overtones of condemning sexual practice, or is simply
exploiting the motif of judgement against the inhabitants of the city
of Sodom.)

For a variation on the schooling of Jesus, see Irenaeus, *Ad. Haer.*
1.20.1. The 'alphabet' incident is discussed more fully in P. Foster,
'Educating Jesus: The Search for a Plausible Context', *Journal for
the Study of the Historical Jesus* 4 (2006): 7–33, esp. 22–5.

On the differences between Greek A and Greek B, see the discussion
in T. Chartrand-Burke, 'The Infancy Gospel of Thomas', in P. Foster
(ed.), *The Non-Canonical Gospels* (London: T&T Clark, 2008),
pp. 126–38.

Elliott notes that 'Possible extracts of PJ [*Protevangelium of James*]
may be found in the chronicle known as the *Barbarus Scakiferi* (or
Excerpta Latina Barbarica) of the fifth century.' See J. K. Elliott,

The Apocryphal New Testament (Oxford: Oxford University Press, 1993), p. 54. The pros and cons of this suggestion have been debated in a series of foreign-language articles listed by Elliott.

For a fuller discussion of the textual problem of Anna's pregnancy in the *Protevangelium of James*, see É. de Strycker, *La forme la plus ancienne du Protévangile de Jacques* (Bruxelles: Société des Bollandistes, 1961), p. 80.

The significance of certain miraculous phenomena surrounding Jesus' birth is discussed in F. Bovon, 'The Suspension of Time in the Protevangelium Jacobi', in B. A. Pearson (ed.), *The Future of Early Christianity: Essays in Honor of Helmut Koester* (Minneapolis, MN: Fortress, 1991), pp. 393–405.

Chapter 4

The initial publication report concerning the codices at Akhmîm is to be found in U. Bouriant, 'Fragments du texte grec du livre d'Énoch et de quelques écrits attribués à saint Pierre', in *Mémoires publié par les membres de la Mission archéologique française au Caire* (t. IX, fasc. 1; Paris, 1892), pp. 93–147.

The *Gospel of Peter*. Peter is mentioned in Eusebius, *H.E.* iii.3.1–3 and vi.12.1–6.

For a recent discussion of the *Gospel of Peter* and docetism, see J. McCant, 'The Gospel of Peter: Docetism Reconsidered', *New Testament Studies* 30 (1984): 258–73.

Perhaps the most famous critic of the more superstitious and miraculous elements of Christianity was the 2nd-century writer Celsus. His *The True Doctrine* is not preserved in its own right, though Origen, in his rebuttal of this work entitled *Contra Celsum*, reproduces large excerpts of it. See H. Chadwick, *Origen: Contra Celsum* (Cambridge: Cambridge University Press, 1953; reprinted, 1965).

The phenomenon of transformation of body size is a feature of a number of early Christian texts. For a fuller discussion, see P. Foster, 'Polymorphic Christology: Its Origins and Development in Early Christianity', *Journal of Theological Studies* 58, Part 1 (2007): 66–99.

J. D. Crossan, *The Cross that Spoke: The Origins of the Passion Narrative* (San Francisco, CA: Harper & Row, 1988). For a fuller discussion of Crossan's theory, see P. Foster, 'The Gospel of Peter', in P. Foster (ed.), *The Non-Canonical Gospels* (London: T&T Clark,

2008), pp. 30–42, esp. 38–40. The quote is from P. A. Mireki, 'Peter, Gospel of', *Anchor Bible Dictionary*, vol. V (New York: Doubleday, 1992), p. 278.

The original publication of Papyrus Oxyrhynchus 840 was presented in B. P. Grenfell and A. S. Hunt (eds.), *The Oxyrhynchus Papyri: Part V* (London: Egypt Exploration Fund, 1907), pp. 1–10; and in a separate pamphlet issued by the same authors, *Fragment of an Uncanonical Gospel* (London: Egypt Exploration Fund, 1908). The translation basically follows that provided by M. J. Kruger, *The Gospel of the Savior: An Analysis of P.Oxy. 840 and Its Place in the Gospel Traditions of Early Christianity* (Leiden: Brill, 2005). See also T. J. Kraus, 'P.Oxy. 840 – Amulet or Miniature Codex? Principal and Additional Remarks on Two Terms', in T. J. Kraus (ed.), *Ad Fonts: Original Manuscripts and Their Significance for Studying Early Christianity – Selected Essays* (Leiden: Brill, 2007), pp. 47–67.

On water baptism, see F. Bovon, 'Fragment Oxyrhynchus 840, Fragment of a Lost Gospel, Witness of an Early Christian Controversy Over Purity', *Journal of Biblical Literature* 119 (2000): 705–28.

On Papyrus Egerton 2, see H. I. Bell and T. C. Skeat, *Fragments of an Unknown Gospel and Other Early Christian Papyri* (London: Trustees, Oxford University Press, 1935), and M. Gronewald, 'Unbekanntes Evangelium oder Evangelienharmonie (Fragment aus dem 'Evangelium Egerton')', in *Kölner Papyri (P.Köln) 6*, ARWAW.PapyCol VII (Opladen, 1987), pp. 136–45. The translations of the fragments of Papyrus Egerton 2 + Papyrus Cologne 255 presented in this chapter are based on both those given by Bell and Skeat, as above, and T. Nicklas, 'Papyrus Egerton 2', in P. Foster (ed.), *The Non-Canonical Gospels* (London: T&T Clark, 2008), pp. 139–49. For Papyrus Egerton 2 in general, there is an invaluable web-based resource: <http://www-user.uni-bremen.de/~wie/Egerton/Egerton_home.html> (accessed 1 September 2008).

For opposing points of view on *nomina sacra*, see L. W. Hurtado, 'The Origin of the *Nomina Sacra*: A Proposal', *Journal of Biblical Literature* 117 (1998): 655–73, and C. M. Tuckett, ' "Nomina Sacra": Yes and No?', in J.-M. Auwers and H. J. Jonge (eds.), *The Biblical Canons*, BETL CLXIII (Leuven: Peeters, 2003), pp. 431–58.

The whole question of the definition of the term 'Jewish–Christian' has resurfaced in recent years as a major issue in biblical scholarship. See the two landmark works: O. Skarsauna and R. Heidar (eds.),

Jewish Believers in Jesus: The Early Centuries (Peabody, MA:
Hendrickson, 2007), esp. pp. 3–55; and M. Jackson-McCabe (ed.),
*Jewish Christianity Reconsidered: Rethinking Ancient Groups and
Texts* (Minneapolis, MN: Fortress, 2007).

The translations of passages cited by various Church fathers from
Jewish–Christian gospels are modified from E. Hennecke and W.
Schneemelcher (eds.), *New Testament Apocrypha*, Volume One:
Gospels and Related Writings, revised edn. (tr. R. McL. Wilson;
Louisville, KY: Westminster/John Knox Press, 1991), pp. 134–178.

Chapter 5

For a discussion of various factors that may have led to Paul's
Damascus Road experience, see J. Ashton, *The Religion of Paul the
Apostle* (New Haven, CT: Yale, 2000), esp. chapter 3.

For a racy description of the events surrounding the passage of Codex
Tchacos, containing the *Gospel of Judas*, from its discovery to its
publication, see H. Krosney, *The Lost Gospel: The Quest for the
Gospel of Judas Iscariot* (Washington, DC: National Geographic,
2006).

The original publication of the English translation of the *Gospel of
Judas* can be found in R. Kasser, M. Meyer, and G. Wurst, with
additional commentary by B. D. Ehrman, *The Gospel of Judas*
(Washington, DC: National Geographic, 2006). See also R. Kasser
and G. Wurst (eds.), *The Gospel of Judas – together with the Letter of
Philip, James and a Book of Allogenes from Codex Tchacos: Critical
Edition* (Washington, DC: National Geographic, 2007), p. 30; and
A. D. DeConick, *The Thirteenth Apostle: What the Gospel of Judas
Really Says* (London: Continuum, 2007). For the various
competing translations, see the alternatives presented in parallel
passages in both Kasser, Meyer, and Wurst, *The Gospel of Judas*,
and DeConick, *The Thirteenth Apostle*.

The most recent critical edition of the *Gospel of Mary* is C. M. Tuckett,
The Gospel of Mary (Oxford: Oxford University Press, 2007). See
also Karen L. King, *The Gospel of Mary of Magdala: Jesus and the
First Woman Apostle* (Santa Rosa, CA: Polebridge Press, 2003).

For the sociology of new religious movements, consult W. S.
Bainbridge, *The Sociology of Religious Movements* (New York:
Routledge, 1997).

Chapter 6

For a discussion of some of the issues surrounding the status of the Nag
Hammadi texts, see S. Emmel, 'Religious Tradition, Textual
Transmission, and the Nag Hammadi Codices', in J. D. Turner and
A. McGuire (eds.), *The Nag Hammadi Library after Fifty Years:
Proceedings of the 1995 Society of Biblical Literature
Commemoration* (Leiden: Brill, 1997), pp. 34–43.

Index

SOCIAL MEDIA
Very Short Introduction

Join our community
www.oup.com/vsi

- Join us online at the official Very Short Introductions **Facebook** page.
- Access the thoughts and musings of our authors with our online **blog**.
- Sign up for our monthly **e-newsletter** to receive information on all new titles publishing that month.
- Browse the full range of Very Short Introductions online.
- Read **extracts** from the Introductions for free.
- Visit our library of **Reading Guides**. These guides, written by our expert authors will help you to question again, why you think what you think.
- If you are a teacher or lecturer you can order inspection copies quickly and simply via our website.

ONLINE CATALOGUE
A Very Short Introduction

Our online catalogue is designed to make it easy to find your ideal Very Short Introduction. View the entire collection by subject area, watch author videos, read sample chapters, and download reading guides.

http://fds.oup.com/www.oup.co.uk/general/vsi/index.html